"Dominik Imseng is a master of oral history. His brilliant piecing together of Volkswagen's classic '60s ad campaign is both illuminating and entertaining."

–Steven Heller, design writer and co-chair MFA Design/Designer as Author and Entrepreneur, School of Visual Arts, NYC

"Dominik Imseng has not only given us a superbly written and well researched history of the unique DDB/VW Beetle relationship of the 1960s and '70s, he has unequivocally reminded us of that oh so brief Golden Age of Advertising when agencies and their clients enjoyed a mutually beneficial business relationship based on trust and respect, rather than inherently false pecuniary ends. That's why Imseng's statement on the very last pages of his book rings so true in today's data-driven environment: *Advertising must do more than simply try to get people's attention–it must try to get their respect.* Amen to that. Recommended reading to everyone, but particularly for those who were not even born in the age of *Think small.*"

–George Parker, author of *MadScam*, *The Ubiquitous Persuaders* and *Confessions of a Mad Man*, www.adscam.typepad.com

"You'd think that everything that could be written about the iconic VW campaign had already been written. But Imseng's book proves this wrong; he delves into the history and the connected (and frequently amusing) anecdotes with wonder and enthusiasm ... as if the work were a newly discovered oeuvre. I can't recommend it highly enough. Get it!"

–Neil French, former Worldwide Creative Director of WPP and author of *Sorry for the Lobsters*

"In an age where the advertising industry seems to care little about the past, this forensic examination of the people and events surrounding DDB's VW campaign is a timely as well as masterful piece of work. At last we have a painstakingly assembled account of what really happened in New York half a century ago in this revolutionary agency. No to mention a clear articulation of the lessons that we would all be wise to remember as we push the advertising discipline into newer and newer territory."

–Richard Huntington, Chief Strategy Officer of
Saatchi & Saatchi London, www.adliterate.com

"Everybody in advertising knows the great Volkswagen ads: *'Lemon, Think small ... Snow Plow ...* er ... the one with the multi-colored Beetle ... and ... er ... erm ...'* Dominik Imseng goes deeper, helping us understand why the Volkswagen campaign changed advertising."

–Dave Dye, *Stuff from the Loft*, www.davedye.com

"In the late 1950s, a handful of rebels transformed the advertising industry. They changed it from a soulless profession obsessed with numbers and blunt messages to a creative profession that produced adverts the public enjoyed consuming. In his book, Dominik Imseng has done a brilliant job of telling the stories of the misfits and geniuses behind that revolution. With any luck, it will inspire a new generation of revolutionaries. The industry appears to have gone full circle."

–Dave Birss, Editor at Large of *The Drum* and author of
A User Guide to the Creative Mind

"If the author's command of his subject is masterful, then his ability to tell it as a story is even more impressive. There are turns of phrase and whole passages here that make my heart sing. That he does all this in English–a language that is not his mother tongue–is awe-inducing. Dominik Imseng is the Joseph Conrad of marketing literature."

–Steve Harrison, author of *How to Do Better Creative Work* and
Changing the World is the Only Fit Work for a Grown Man

"Damn good book."

–Ed McCabe, Co-Founder, President,
Worldwide Creative Director of Scali, McCabe, Sloves, Inc.

Which was your favorite?

You are looking at the winners.

The famous Printers' Ink executive survey voted Volkswagen advertising the best in 1960.

The reasons?

Listen to the voters: "Refreshing," "Off-beat believability," "Concentration on fact," "Sales results (just look at all the bugs on the road.)"

The award was made not just for one ad but for the entire series. This is important to an advertiser. It means that ad after ad worked hard for him. It means that the agency which created these ads is able to make every ad count.

This agency—Doyle Dane Bernbach—has sustained the same continuity of provocative advertising in its work for Polaroid Cameras, El Al Airlines, Ohrbach's, Chemstrand, Schenley, French Government Tourist, Yardley, Coffee of Colombia, Thom McAn, ABC-TV Network, Dreyfus Fund, Lane Furniture and others.

The record is quite clear. In another survey taken last year by News Front magazine, advertising experts were asked to choose the 10 best ads of the decade 1950 to 1960. Of the 10 best campaigns chosen, one agency had created four. That agency is:

Doyle Dane Bernbach.

Ugly
Is
Only
Skin-
Deep

The Story of the Ads
That Changed the World

Dominik Imseng

This book is the largely expanded version of
Think Small. The Story of the World's Greatest Ad,
published by Full Stop Press in 2011.

Matador
9 Priory Business Park,
Wistow Road, Kibworth Beauchamp,
Leicestershire. LE8 0RX
Tel: 0116 279 2299
Email: books@troubador.co.uk
Web: www.troubador.co.uk/matador
Twitter: @matadorbooks

ISBN 978 1785893 179

British Library Cataloguing in Publication Data.
A catalogue record for this book is available from the British Library.

Printed and bound by CPI Group (UK) Ltd, Croydon, CR0 4YY
Typeset in 11pt Aldine401 BT by Troubador Publishing Ltd, Leicester, UK

To Anna & Raoul
and Petra, Finian & Linus

"All of us who professionally use the mass media are the shapers of society. We can vulgarize that society. We can brutalize it. Or we can help lift it onto a higher level."

–Bill Bernbach

CONTENTS

FOREWORD

By Carl H. Hahn

I n the course of its history, the Volkswagen Group has acquired merit and recognition in many areas. Less well known is that VW also triggered a revolution in the world of advertising.

It began in the summer of 1959 in a little-known ad agency called Doyle Dane Bernbach on a New York City backyard. DDB had just won the Volkswagen account to market the Beetle in the U.S., with a ridiculously small budget.

The agency managed to fascinate America with an entirely new way of advertising and redeem it from the monotony of the traditional ads of that period, which tended to show elegant ladies and gentlemen in front of expensive villas in beautiful parks. The ads for the Beetle were refreshingly different, as distinctive as the car itself: sober in appearance, almost plain, but always original and entertaining, with a dash of humor and disarming honesty. Ads like *Think small* or *Lemon* made understatement socially acceptable and gave the Beetle cult status. In 1999, *Advertising Age* voted *Think small* the best ad of the 20th century.

By collaborating with DDB, Volkswagen not only had the lowest advertising costs per vehicle, but also achieved U.S. sales that helped grow VW in a dimension previously unimaginable for a European car manufacturer. As the advertising philosophy developed for the American market was universally applicable, the campaign secured the Volkswagen Group a uniform appearance. As a result, Volkswagen's product strategy, combined with Bill Bernbach's inexhaustible creativity, revolutionized the advertising world. More than half a century later, DDB still remains closely associated with Volkswagen–a unique collaboration in this fast-paced industry.

I am pleased that this book recalls the merits of VW in the field of advertising. It is also important for me to acknowledge the work of Doyle Dane Bernbach and not let fall into oblivion the spirit that inspired its team.

DDB has succeeded in a unique way to make the Beetle a symbol of quality and durability. The VW campaign set standards across all industries and is leading the way in the advertising world to this day.

Professor Carl H. Hahn (b. 1926) began his career at Volkswagen in 1954 as assistant to then CEO Heinrich Nordhoff. From 1959 to 1964, he was CEO of Volkswagen of America and thus the original client of the campaign presented in this book. Hahn eventually acted as CEO of the Volkswagen Group until his retirement in 1992.

INTRODUCTION

By Amir Kassaei

Every industry has its supernova–a moment in time when something happens that changes everything, elevating everything to a higher level and inspiring people to go on a new path and make their own mark.

The supernova of advertising was the campaign for the Volkswagen Beetle, created by Doyle Dane Bernbach in the 1960s.

From that moment on, advertising became a different game.

All of a sudden, creativity in marketing and communications could not only seduce people in an intelligent way, but also move them and have an impact on society, art, music, design and everything else.

Until today, anyone who thinks about innovative, intelligent and game-changing advertising–and anyone who tries to create it–is inspired and led by the principles of the Creative Revolution.

And even with digital technology, which has changed and disrupted a lot of the aspects of our business and will continue to do so even more, the best advertising will always be based on a genuine human insight and the talent to deliver it in a fresh and magical way.

This is the legacy of Bill Bernbach and of his agency DDB. I am very happy and honored to work here, and to try and live the values of the Creative Revolution.

And I will make a bet: even in generations from now, people will look back and refer to the Volkswagen campaign as the bar of creative advertising–and be inspired by it.

Amir Kassaei (b. 1968), Chief Creative Officer of DDB Worldwide, was born in Iran, raised in Austria and educated in France. He is one of the most lauded creatives in the world, working on brands such as Adidas, Apple, Coca-Cola, McDonald's, Nike, Reebok–and Volkswagen.

The front, the back, the side–the original Volkswagen is the most iconic car ever. But it wasn't German engineering only that made the Beetle unique. It was a Manhattan advertising agency, too.

Created in 1959 by Doyle Dane Bernbach and continued through the '60s and early '70s, the campaign for the Volkswagen Beetle is considered the best of all time. More than just promoting a car, it promoted a new kind of advertising: simple, charming, intelligent and–most of all–honest.

In this book, we'll retrace the creation of Doyle Dane Bernbach, sneered at by the big players on Madison Avenue because of the 'ethnic' background of its founders and employees who were mostly Jewish.

You'll then learn how the agency won the Volkswagen account and how an unlikely creative team set the tone for the most admired campaign in advertising history.

Finally, we'll look at the evolution of the Volkswagen campaign and how it managed to convince more and more Americans that smaller was better.

In fact, the Volkswagen campaign didn't only fundamentally change the ethos of advertising–it also helped trigger the cultural revolution of the 1960s.

Ready for the ride? Then get into the Beetle.

Dominik Imseng   *July 14, 2016*

"I want those rules broken"

Bill Bernbach discovers the power of great ideas

S tanding a mere 5'7" and soft-spoken, Bill Bernbach didn't look or sound like he would change the world. And yet he did.

Born in New York City on August 13, 1911, as one of four children, Bernbach would joke that his parents were too poor to give him a middle name. But that wasn't true: his father Jacob–a Jewish immigrant from Eastern Europe–was a successful designer of women's clothes.

Little Bill enjoyed reading and playing the piano. He developed an early appreciation for art and had a natural talent for writing. As a young man, Bernbach attended New York University where he received a bachelor's degree in English literature in 1933. At least that's what he would later tell reporters to give himself the aura of an artist. In reality, Bernbach graduated–somewhat more prosaically–from New York University's School of Commerce, Accounts and Finance, obtaining a bachelor's degree in commercial science with a major in marketing.

Either way, entering the world of work in 1933–right in the middle of the Great Depression–made it very hard to get a job. Bernbach eventually found one in the mailroom of Schenley Distillers in Midtown Manhattan, with a meager salary of $16 a week. The office boy quickly became the head of the mailroom, but had other ambitions, with a keen desire to break into advertising.

In between deliveries, Bernbach wrote ads for Schenley's various liquor brands and sent the one he liked best–for American Cream Whiskey–to Lord & Thomas, Schenley's respected advertising agency. He received no response, but sometime later, Bernbach opened up *The New York Times* and found his ad idea produced, the words exactly as he had written them. With the self-confidence that would become his trademark, Bernbach went to Lord & Thomas to get his letter back. Having proved his intellectual property to the secretary of Lewis Rosenstiel, Schenley's then President, the aspiring copywriter was given a raise and reassigned to the marketing and advertising department–much to the annoyance of its head, one Mr. Greenlee, who told him, "Don't think because you went to college you're going to be a big shot around here."

"I don't think anything about my going to college," Bernbach replied. "I just don't want it to be held against me."[1]

It wasn't long before the young man became the protégé of yet another powerful Schenley figure: Chairman of the Board Grover Whalen. The prominent businessman and politician made Bernbach his personal assistant and took him along on a business trip to Washington, instructing Bill on the art of tipping and teaching him a little savoir-faire.

When Whalen left Schenley in 1935 to run the 1939 New York World's Fair, his assistant went along. First Bernbach worked in the Fair's PR department, producing articles and brochures, then he started writing speeches for Whalen and civic dignitaries who visited the Fair. His job would have a major influence on Bernbach's future advertising philosophy: not only did he learn how language could be used to effectively persuade people–he also learnt that people are persuaded more easily if you respect their intelligence.

As a young man already, Bill Bernbach was convinced that people are persuaded more easily if you respect their intelligence.

After the Fair closed in 1940, Bernbach was unemployed for a full year. With only his newly-wed wife's small pay as a receptionist, the young couple's financial situation became so bad that Bill had to ask his parents for help. But they refused, angry about their son's marriage to a non-Jewish girl. On realizing the couple's despair, a Schenley executive, who was friendly with them, recommended Bill to William Weintraub who had just started an advertising agency, with Schenley Distillers as one of its first clients.

"I have three guys applying for this copy job," Weintraub told Bernbach, "why don't you write me a letter telling me why you should have it?"

"I don't know why I should have it," Bernbach replied. "I don't even know if I'm equipped."

"Why don't you write the letter anyway?"[2]

The letter must have been good: at age 30, Bill Bernbach landed his first real job in advertising.

PAUL RAND WAS 27 when Bernbach joined the Weintraub agency, yet the graphic designer was already a star.

Born Peretz Rosenbaum in the Brooklyn section of New York City, Rand was enrolled at Pratt Institute and Parsons The New School for Design, but was mainly self-taught. He would spend his days in bookshops flicking through *Gebrauchsgrafik* and *Commercial Art*, two European graphic arts magazines that introduced Rand to the modernist art school called the Bauhaus, founded by Walter Gropius in Weimar, Germany, in 1919. With artist lecturers such as Max Bill, Marcel Breuer, Lyonel Feininger, Wassily Kandinsky, Paul Klee, László Moholy-Nagy or Piet Mondrian, the unadorned Bauhaus style–seeking complete harmony between function and form–would have a worldwide impact on art, architecture, graphic design, interior design, industrial design and typography. This was despite Hitler shutting down the school in 1933, considering it a stronghold of communist propaganda.

In 1936, Rand was hired as a freelance designer for the quarterly men's fashion magazine *Apparel Arts*. The freshness of his page design and Rand's talent for transforming ordinary photographs into explosive compositions quickly earned him a full-time job plus an offer to work for the men's magazine *Esquire*. On top of this, Rand started to create covers for the cultural magazine *Direction*, which he designed without charge in exchange for artistic freedom. It was with these radically modernist covers–especially the December 1940 issue, looking like it had been wrapped in barbed wire–that Rand's work began to receive international recognition.

In 1941, the brilliant graphic mind took on yet another challenge: when William Weintraub started his own ad agency, Rand joined him as head of art. From the beginning, his work changed the look and feel of American advertising. Stark, witty

The brilliant graphic mind Paul Rand made
Bernbach realize the importance of art direction.

and eye-catching, Rand's ads did more than simply illustrate the headlines or slogans of copywriters–they were ideas in themselves, *visual* ideas.

Back then, this was something completely new. Traditionally, ads were conceived by copywriters who turned the advertising proposition–what the client wanted to communicate–into a headline and body copy. An account executive handed their typescript along with a drawing of the suggested layout to a 'commercial artist' or 'visualizer' to create the final ad. Since the copywriter and the commercial artist were usually working on separate floors, the two often wouldn't even know each other.

Rand completely ignored this traditional gap between 'conceptual' copywriters and 'executional' art directors. This impressed Bernbach since he understood that treating the art director as an equal would make perfect sense. Bob Gage, another ingenious graphic mind whom Bernbach would later work with, knew why: "Two people who respect each other sit in the same room for a length of time and arrive at a state of … free association, where the mention of one idea will

Paul Rand's radically modernist cover for the 1940 Christmas issue of the cultural magazine Direction.

Paul Rand's ads did more than simply illustrate the headlines of copywriters–they were visual ideas.

lead to another idea, and then to another."[3] The art director might suggest a headline, the writer a visual. The entire ad is conceived as a whole, in a kind of ping pong between disciplines. The result, according to advertising historian Stephen Fox, is a "combination of the visual and the words coming together and forming a third bigger thing."[4]

Blending their talents on ads for the aperitif Dubonnet, the milliner Lee Hats and the department store Ohrbach's, Bernbach and Rand became close friends, visiting art galleries and museums during lunch breaks and talking about the need for a new kind of advertising that would always be focused on one great thing–a powerful *idea*.

The famous art director George Lois, who knew both Rand and Bernbach very well, recalls:

> *"The seed for advertising's Creative Revolution was planted when Bernbach met Rand at the Weintraub agency. Here was an art director who not only wrote and designed his own ads–he also didn't take any shit from anybody. Meeting Rand, Bernbach had an epiphany about the whole creative process. He realized that advertising could be ten times better if a talented writer works with a talented art director. In fact, I told Rand once, 'When Bill Bernbach met you, it was like Columbus discovering America.'"*[5]

And vice versa: "This was my first encounter with a copywriter," Rand said, "who understood visual ideas and who didn't come in with a yellow copy pad and a preconceived notion of what the layout should look like."[6]

The remarkable fruits of Rand and Bernbach's collaboration are still included in just about every book on the history of graphic design. A particular favorite is *Mechanized Mules of Victory*, a spiral-bound brochure with embossed cover for the armored vehicle manufacturer The Autocar Company. Produced in 1942, it contains a dozen blocks of perfectly set copy written by Bernbach, explaining how the company's anti-tank vehicles and troop carriers were "helping to build for America a motorized Armada such as the world has never seen."[7]

Shortly after, Bernbach was drafted to serve in the U.S. army, but the examining doctor at Fort Eustis, Virginia, found the new recruit's pulse so elevated that he doubted Bill would survive military training. (Ever the image maker, Bernbach later embellished the truth, telling reporters that his stint in the U.S. army had lasted much longer.) The ad man returned to New York City, where Arthur Fatt and Larry Valenstein–founders of the successful Jewish agency Grey–hired him as a copywriter. After winning a host of new clients, Bernbach became Vice President in charge of copy and art in 1945.

Bernbach's first creative team at Grey (and later at DDB): Phyllis Robinson (copy) and Bob Gage (art).

Bernbach wanted to make the copy/art partnership he had so enjoyed with Rand the pillar of Grey's creative process (since then, the so-called 'creative team' has become industry standard). The first to combine their talents were Phyllis Robinson, formerly a copywriter in Grey's sales promotion department, and Bob Gage, a brilliant graphic designer whom Paul Rand had advised Bernbach to hire. Gage noted:

> *"The night before I had the appointment with Bernbach, I removed everything from my portfolio that showed any compromise. Bill went through the work, liked it, and I got the job. Before I left, we discussed the future of advertising. How he saw it. How I saw it. His enthusiasm and his being so articulate had a profound effect upon me. I had at last found someone who not just tolerated new ideas, but demanded them."[8]*

Grey's clients were mostly Jewish retail outlets on Seventh Avenue. The low-priced department store Ohrbach's–an

Rosser Reeves, whose brutal repetition of
a 'Unique Selling Proposition' (USP)
Bernbach absolutely wanted to avoid.

account Bernbach had already worked on at the Weintraub agency–proved to be a particularly productive client. Constantly demanding new ideas and giving instant feedback on their sales power, Ohrbach's became, as it were, Bernbach's Research & Development account–a playing field for the creation of clever, witty ads, with sharp, conversational copy instead of advertising jargon, and clean minimalism instead of cluttered layouts.

There was something else Bernbach wanted to avoid: fellow ad man Rosser Reeves' brutal repetition of a 'Unique Selling Proposition' (USP), getting a "message into the heads of the most people at the lowest possible cost."[9] Seeing the fruits of this advertising philosophy–especially Reeves' mind-numbing TV commercials for the pain reliever Anacin (*Fast, fast, incredibly fast relief!*) from the 1950s–Bernbach was reminded of Evan Llewellyn Evans, the grotesque soap tycoon in former copywriter Frederic Wakeman's novel *The Hucksters*, turned into a popular movie in 1947. "Beautee Soap! Beautee Soap! Beautee Soap!", Evans shouts in one scene. "Repeat it

Maybe the most annoying ad in advertising history:
Rosser Reeves' TV commercial for the pain reliever Anacin.
Watch it on tinyurl.com/ugly-anacin

till it comes out of their ears! Repeat it till they say it in their sleep! Irritate them, irritate, irritate till they never forget it, then knock them dead!"

What's more, "ads were tested before they ran, while they ran and after they ran, in an attempt to make sure the sales message meant all things, to all people," notes British advertising great Alfredo Marcantonio. "More often than not, though, the work that resulted meant nothing to anyone, except of course the agency and client involved."[10]

For Bernbach, knowing the right thing to say was only the starting point–it was *how* you say it that made for an effective ad, and "if breaking every rule in the world is going to achieve that," he demanded, "I want those rules broken."[11]

By the late 1940s, though, Grey had grown so big that bureaucracy and procedural constraints produced an allegiance to science rather than art.

Which is why, in May 1947, Bernbach sent a memo to his bosses that could be considered the manifesto of advertising's Creative Revolution:

"I'm worried that we're going to fall into the trap of bigness ... that we're going to worship techniques instead of substance ... There are a lot of great technicians in advertising ... But there's one little rub. Advertising is fundamentally persuasion and persuasion happens to be not a science, but an art ..."

"Let us blaze new trails," Bernbach concluded. "Let us prove to the world that good taste, good art, good writing can be good selling."[12]

Arthur Fatt and Larry Valenstein ignored Bernbach's memo.

AT GREY, BERNBACH WORKED closely with Ned Doyle, a Vice President of business accounts. Ten years Bill's senior, Doyle–of Irish descent–was a former star quarterback and served as a captain in Marine Corps Aviation during World War II. Highly masculine and good-looking, he was the complete opposite of Bernbach who–according to famous ad woman Mary Wells Lawrence–was not much to look at, with a "wary half-smile, cow's-milk eyes, pale skin, [and] soft shoulders."[13] But there was one thing Doyle and Bernbach shared: their deep distaste for the conformity of Madison Avenue.

The street lined with ad agencies, nick-named 'Ulcer Gulch,' was populated by those who would come to be called 'The Men in the Gray Flannel Suit,' described by Sloan Wilson in his 1955 bestseller of the same title. A joke of the period says it all:

"What time is it?", a client asks.

"What time would you like it to be?", the agency man answers.

"Tales of a client admiring a pony for his daughter and the agency account executive delivering said pony to the client's home the next day were not apocryphal," remembered well-known ad man Phil Dusenberry who started out as a copywriter in the early 1960s.[14] This devotion to brown-nosing–the litany of persuasive client gifts even included women–gave advertising an extremely bad reputation. TV shows and movies mocked the account executive desperately trying not to offend his clients, and it wasn't just the 'suits' who had a negative image. *The Hucksters,* again, best reflects the era's perception of advertising creatives, with copywriter Victor Norman, played by Clark Gable, knocking out a cheap, catchy slogan before enjoying another amorous adventure.

Bill Bernbach could not have been more different. Alongside Ned Doyle, he was ever-ready to dump clients when they didn't follow agency recommendations the same way they would accept the advice of a lawyer or the prescription of a doctor. Ned Doyle even fantasized ways of showing unwilling clients the door. "You go to a hardware store and buy a power mower," he suggested to an account executive who was complaining about a difficult client, "then shove it up his ass and turn on the power."[15]

Encouraged by Nathan M. Ohrbach, the founder of the department store, who promised Bernbach his account and even proposed to pay his bills in advance, so that the young agency would have enough money, Bernbach and Doyle began talking to Herbert Strauss, another Vice President at Grey, about starting their own business. When Strauss dropped out– he was offered the position of Grey President–Doyle contacted Maxwell Dane, an old friend and tennis partner who had been the advertising and promotion manager of *Look* magazine before starting his own small ad agency in 1944. After a few discussions the deal was closed: Doyle would get forty percent of the shares and run the account side, Dane would have twenty percent and handle administration and finance, and Bernbach would be given forty percent and free rein over the creative department.

The founders of DDB: Bill Bernbach, Ned Doyle and Maxwell Dane.

Doyle Dane Bernbach opened shop at the address of Dane's former agency: 350 Madison Avenue, a floor and a half above the last elevator stop. Phyllis Robinson noted: "It was June 1st, 1949. I tend to remember important dates. The day I was born, the day I had a child, and the day DDB started."[16]

It was also the first year that a strange little car from Germany was imported to the U.S.

CHAPTER 2

"New York is eating it up"

Doyle Dane Bernbach makes people love ads again

"There were twelve people in all including the telephone operator," remembered Phyllis Robinson in 1969. "The creative department was Bernbach at the head, Bob Gage as head art director, myself as copy chief. I had no one else at all, and Bob Gage had just very few assistants, paste-up people and so forth, that he needed to physically put the work together."[1]

Ned Doyle, Maxwell Dane and Bill Bernbach had flipped a coin to settle the order of their names in the agency title, after which Bernbach made the likely apocryphal statement: "Nothing will ever come between us. Not even punctuation."[2]

The three men were also united by their somewhat problematic heritage: Bernbach and Dane were Jewish, and Doyle was Roman Catholic.

This raised a lot of eyebrows back then, because in the 1950s, Madison Avenue agencies such as Batten, Barton, Durstine & Osborn (BBDO), Foote, Cone & Belding (FCB), J. Walter Thompson or McCann-Erickson were almost entirely staffed by White Anglo-Saxon Protestants (WASPs).

There were some Jews working in research departments, mostly psychologists and sociologists who had fled Austria and Germany in the 1930s, but hardly any in management, except for Jewish-owned agencies like Grey, primarily located on

Seventh Avenue, next to their Jewish clients. Some advertisers–such as Lawrence Jones of Four Roses Whiskey–even explicitly demanded that no Jews work on their account. This 'ethnic' segregation was something that creative veteran Jerry Della Femina remembered well when he wrote his hilarious book *From Those Wonderful Folks Who Gave You Pearl Harbor*: Protestant ad agencies "monopolized all the large advertising accounts (cars, food, cigarettes, soft drinks, beer). The other, smaller accounts (dress manufacturers, shoes, underwear, small retail stores) were regulated to tiny, 'Jewish' ad agencies."[3]

Phil Dusenberry noted yet another characteristic of the advertising industry in those days: "Relationships ... used to be the Good Old Boy network, East Coast division–guys who had gone to Princeton together, enjoyed three-martini lunches and met for a round of golf in the middle of the week. The primary focus was on the social aspects of a relationship. This was the glue that held it all together."[4] (Think of the account men Roger Sterling and Pete Campbell in the TV series *Mad Men*, whose primary job is to humor clients.)

What's more, the history of the agency business started when newspapers announced that they would give a kickback to anyone who got a company to run an ad. To set himself apart from the competition, one of these agents decided to offer free advice on how to write and design the ads. He was quickly copied, and as agencies grew bigger, these creative services became more important. Since they were not the core business, though, the rank of copywriters and visualizers was clearly defined. They were not the ones running the show. They were not the 'business people.'

At Doyle Dane Bernbach, things were completely different: not only had the balance of power shifted from the account executives to the creatives–DDB was strikingly multicultural in its copywriters and art directors, employing

Bill Bernbach. Inspiring, encouraging–but also frightening.
"He mowed everybody around him down and out of sight,"
remembers creative legend Mary Wells Lawrence.

a number of second-generation Jews, Italians, Greeks and
other minorities who were willing to leave the 'ethnic ghetto'
of their parents, but whom, despite their obvious talent, no
established Madison Avenue agency would have hired.

In the loosest sense, Doyle Dane Bernbach became what
the U.S.A. had been for the immigrant parents of these
unconventional recruits: a place for the homeless who yearned
to breathe free.

There is something else that made DDB's hiring policy
special, notes Alfredo Marcantonio: "As the *Mad Men* series
all too regularly demonstrates, a New York agency's female
staff were far more likely to have their bottoms pinched
than their brains picked."[5] With Phyllis Robinson, however,
Bernbach hired a woman as head of copy, who in turn would
employ more female copywriters, such as Paula Green, Lore
Parker, Judy Protas, Rita Selden and Mary Wells Lawrence.
In addition, DDB drew on the graduates of art schools and

English departments, instead of the traditional economics or law alumni, and with this, a new less structured business culture broke through the rigid corporate setting of traditional Madison Avenue agencies.

Phyllis Robinson observed this clearly: "The mood from the beginning was very informal. We talked together, ate together, compared ads."[6]

> *"Novelists would come and say, 'Is there some way you could make use of me?' One day, a young, blond-haired designer came in and showed me his illustrations. I thought it was interesting but we didn't have any jobs for him. A week later, I saw one of the same illustrations published in the corner of the newspaper, signed Andy Warhol."*[7]

Always in the middle of this "wonderful club,"[8] as Robinson described it, was Bill Bernbach, shirt sleeves rolled up, smoking, walking around the creative department, making the visuals even bigger and the headlines even shorter, inspiring, encouraging–but also frightening. Bernbach "communicated such a powerful inner presence," remembers Mary Wells Lawrence, that:

> *"… he mowed everybody around him down and out of sight. In his peak years many people were afraid of him. I was; I didn't want to get too close. There was something volcanic, something unsettling going on; it was a little like being in the company of Mao or Che or the young Fidel. Many of us had hiding places at the agency where we could avoid him. One of his top talents … said he used to go to work at dawn to get his work done … and would be long gone before Bill put a foot into the place. It is true that even some of the surest men who were close to Bill drank more than they should have."*[9]

The famous copywriter Bob Levenson recalled another aspect of Bernbach's personality that instilled fear among DDB employees:

> *"When you were an art director or a copywriter and Bernbach was the creative director, you really did not want to have him turn something down. Because sometimes, he would get nasty about it. If you did an ad or a campaign and he turned it down, you would go back to your office, put yourself together and do another one. If he turned that one down again, he would usually say something like, 'Don't come back here until you have something smart to show me.' That would kill you."[10]*

There's one anecdote that illustrates Bernbach's super-sized ego: stepping out of the agency on a sunny day, someone remarked to him, "What beautiful weather."

"Thank you," Bernbach replied.[11]

(David Ogilvy remembered once having Bill Bernbach and Rosser Reeves as his lunch guests. "Bill lectured us both as if we were trainees at his agency," the Scottish ad legend recalled.[12])

The fact that this small, soft-spoken man was able to become such an awe-inspiring figure in just a couple of years was perhaps in part because of his upbringing.

Bernbach was raised in two cultures at once–the Old World culture of his Jewish parents, who had emigrated from Europe at the end of the nineteenth century, and the bustling New York City of the 1920s and 1930s. What was true at home wasn't necessarily true outside, and vice versa.

From this experience, Bernbach must have developed a healthy dose of skepticism and mental flexibility. He was able to rethink routines and come up with new ways of doing things. Ready to question the rules, procedures, manners and

I found out about... Joan

Ohrbach's

This ad for Ohrbach's proved
so popular that the department store
received hundreds of requests for copies.

hierarchies of Madison Avenue, Bernbach came to realize: many of the maxims accepted as 'good practice' are, in fact, myths that only prevent true progress.

So he became a non-conformist. Someone who looks at the world around him and asks, "Is there a way I could improve it?" Someone who drives change and creativity. Someone who decides to speak out his beliefs and stand up for his ideals.

DOYLE DANE BERNBACH grew quickly, with most clients being companies owned by Jewish American entrepreneurs, such as Hess (an upscale department store in Allentown, PA), clothing manufacturers BVD Underwear and Wear-Right Gloves and 'ethnic' food products Goodman's Matzos and Hygrade's Kosher All Beef Frankfurters.

From the start, the agency had a clear philosophy, said Bob Levenson: "We would only present one campaign. Maybe that was cockiness on our part, but it seemed like faith in our work, we used to say, 'Sorry, we're not going to show you our wastebasket.'"[13]

Another principle of DDB–or Doyle Dane as the creative shop was referred to by the industry back then–was that it was up to the agency to decide which message was most effective and which campaign communicated it best. Bernbach put it this way:

> *"We think we will never know as much about a product as a client. After all, he sleeps and breathes his product. By the same token, we firmly believe that he can't know as much about advertising. Because we live and breathe that all day long."[14]*

The biggest showcase for DDB in those early years was the continuation of Bernbach's work for Ohrbach's, which was by now making the department store as popular as Macy's, but with only one thirtieth of its budget. (This holds another lesson for marketers today: it's not about how much you spend–it's about how big your idea is.) Two of DDB's most famous Ohrbach's ads were produced in 1957 and 1958. The first one showed a man carrying a cardboard cutout of a well-dressed woman under the headline, *Bring in your wife and just a few dollars … we will give you a new woman.* In the second ad, a cat wearing a stylish hat and showing off an elegant cigarette holder peers out under the headline, *I found out about Joan*, while in the witty copy beneath, a 'catty' gossip reveals that her neighbor's expensive looking style comes, in fact, from Ohrbach's. Today, with H & M or Zara, the concept of 'high fashion at low prices' is standard, but back then, this was the first time such an idea had been raised. In fact, the ad proved so popular that the department store received hundreds of requests for copies.

Another early client was the Brooklyn-based bakery Levy's. DDB created a print ad with the headline, *New York is eating it up!*, set over three slices of bread–the first slice with one bite, the second with four, and the third where only a crust is left.

A visually intriguing ad, from 1952, for the Brooklyn-based bakery Levy's. The art director was Bob Gage.

This ad for El Al, done in 1957, ignored the airline industry's number one rule: never show the sea because people are afraid of falling into it.

Just as visually intriguing was an ad for El Al Israel Airlines, done in 1957. It showed the torn away photograph of a turbulent sea, revealing a bit of white page and the headline, *Starting Dec. 23 the Atlantic Ocean will be 20% smaller.* (El Al was the first airline to fly nonstop across the Atlantic, saving you twenty percent of time.) The ad not only broke from conventional airline advertising that merely featured airplanes or flight attendants, it also ignored the industry's number one rule: never show the sea because people are afraid of falling into it.

El Al–almost unknown before–tripled its sales, and the 'torn ocean ad' became heavily talked about in the trade press. Bob Levenson remembered seeing the ad on the train one morning and thinking, "The hell with what I'm doing now– I've got to go to work for DDB."[15] Thirty years later, he still considered the ad one of the best examples of "pure Bernbach:

the words and pictures are stunning and inseparable," and "the advantage to the customer is piercingly clear … presented in a way that no one could pass by."[16]

The success of these campaigns and a slew of others–all making the respective advertising budget look much bigger thanks to a great idea and its superb execution–led to more and more clients calling. With the result that in 1959, ten years after going into business, Doyle Dane Bernbach was billing around $27,500,000 and had been able to move out of its early cramped premises into a larger space on 11 West 42nd Street.

But there was still one thing missing to make the agency a true threat to the establishment on Madison Avenue.

A 'real' account.

A hard goods account.

A car account.

CHAPTER 3

"This isn't worth a damn"

The Volkswagen rises from the ashes of war

The car that was to become an icon of the peace movement began life as a swastika on wheels.

When Hitler came to power in 1933, German motorization was lagging behind America and much of Europe with only one car per fifty citizens. So the 'Führer' immediately launched an ambitious program to bring cars to the people. He proclaimed:

> *"The first step … is to do away with the idea that a motorcar is a luxury. What I want is not a car for two hundred thousand or three hundred thousand [people] who can afford it, but a car which six million or seven million [people] can afford."*[1]

Hitler's vision of the automobile all good Aryans should be able to own was well defined: the car would seat a complete family, run about forty miles per gallon, cost no more than a medium-range motorcycle (around 1000 Reichsmark, the average monthly income of the period being 130 Reichsmark)– and be adaptable for military use.

Ferdinand Porsche, a former technical director of the Austro Daimler Car Company and maybe the greatest automotive engineer ever, was the man to make Hitler's dream come true. The Nazi leisure organization *Kraft durch*

A very happy Adolf Hitler admiring Ferdinand Porsche's miniature model of the Volkswagen.

Freude ('Strength through Joy') or *KdF* created prototypes of the *KdF-Wagen*, tested by SS men from 1936 onwards. These vehicles already featured the Beetle's trademark engine in the back, the placement of which had been found to improve traction by distributing the car's weight more evenly.

In May 1938, Hitler laid the cornerstone for the *Volkswagenwerk*. The factory was Europe's largest and most sophisticated to date, surrounded by a new city built for the workers. However, in the initial phases, only a few hundred civilian cars rolled off the production line, reserved for the Nazi elite or allies such as Mussolini or Emperor Hirohito. Instead, the *Volkswagenwerk* produced—mostly through slave labor— around fifty thousand military vehicles known as *Kübelwagen*, the equivalent to the U.S. Jeep. The later *Schwimmkübel*, an amphibious version, could be driven straight into the water where it became a boat with a propeller at the back. Other military versions of the *KdF-Wagen* included a *Kübelwagen* with metal wheels fit for railroad tracks and even a half-track (two wheels at the front and tank-like tracks at the back) for

Ferdinand Porsche, father of the Volkswagen
and maybe the greatest automotive engineer ever.

the deep snows of Russia. Yet, it was in the Sahara that the *Kübelwagen* found its greatest admirer: Field Marshal Erwin Rommel. His military Beetle was so light that it didn't set off the explosion when the legendary Desert Fox strayed into a minefield. Rommel personally thanked Porsche for saving his life.

By the end of World War II, the *Volkswagenwerk*–in what the British occupation army now called Wolfsburg–was almost completely bombed-out. Allied governments and various car companies refused to take over the plant–one Ford executive famously said, "I don't think what we're being offered here is worth a damn"[2]–and the factory was returned to the government of the newly founded German federal-state of Lower Saxony in 1948.

The British left Heinrich 'Heinz' Nordhoff in charge of the *Volkswagenwerk*. A former Opel executive and one of the most visionary CEOs ever, Nordhoff recognized the potential in the U.S. car market as soon as production of

*One of the many military
versions of the Volkswagen:
the* Kübelwagen.

*Heinrich 'Heinz' Nordhoff.
The Volkswagen CEO decided
to conquer the U.S. market,
selling two Beetles in 1949 and
120,000 in 1959.*

the civilian Beetle began in 1949. The Volkswagen, however, was still known as the 'Führer's car,' thus the first vehicles imported to the U.S. weren't met with much enthusiasm. Furthermore, the Beetle's small size and compact design did little to attract Americans who were falling in love with huge automobiles that looked like airplanes–and were almost the same size.

Nevertheless, the small car won a few favorable articles in magazines such as *Popular Mechanics* and *Reader's Digest*, and Volkswagen of America managed to establish and quickly expand its customer base. From just two cars sold in 1949, annual registrations rose to 80,000 by 1957. This increase in sale was no surprise: the Volkswagen was a cheap and reliable car, which coped well in rough terrains. It also had excellent gas mileage, an air-cooled engine that couldn't overheat or freeze, and replacement parts were inexpensive. In addition, the growth of American suburbia created the need for two cars per family, and in choosing the inexpensive Volkswagen, customers freed up cash for other fashionable purchases.

As annual sales reached over 100,000 by 1958, American manufacturers could no longer dismiss the Volkswagen as a freak for freaks. Furthermore, surveys suggested that the average Volkswagen buyer was not only younger than the average American car buyer, but also better educated and in possession of a higher disposable income.

It came as no surprise that Chrysler, Ford and General Motors all announced that in late 1959 and early 1960 they would launch small cars, too. These were the so-called 'compacts': Chevrolet, a division of General Motors, produced the Corvair; Plymouth, a division of Chrysler, the Valiant; and Ford released the Falcon (the company still recovering from what may well be the biggest flop in marketing history ever: the family car Edsel, launched in 1957 and completely ignored by the public, although Ford had invested a gigantic $250 million, $30 million of which on advertising alone). The marketing budget behind each of these launches was $10 million. "Volkswagen will be out of business in this country in two years," boasted Chevrolet's General Manager Ed Cole.[3]

In preparation for the Detroit-based counterattack, Volkswagen of America decided that they had to invest in product advertising. Up to this point, they had only run corporate ads produced by Volkswagen's own advertising department in Wolfsburg, showing sales figures and the number of countries in which the Beetle was being sold. A low-profile communications strategy that had been approved by the visionary 1960s ad man Howard Luck Gossage, as his widow Sally Kemp remembers:

*Prior to hiring DDB, Volkswagen's own advertising department
in Wolfsburg produced low-profile corporate ads like this one.*

*"Volkswagen came to [Howard] ... and they wanted him to
do the advertising ... [but] he looked at the car and then told
them, 'You know, this product is like a Hershey Bar ... You
don't need to advertise this ... It's going to sell itself.'"[4]*

With the impeding launch of Detroit's 'compacts,' however,
the time had come to start looking for an ad agency again, and
to do this, Wolfsburg sent over a new man.

CARL H. HAHN, the newly appointed General Manager
of Volkswagen of America, took over on January 1, 1959,
at the age of only 32, but the brilliant economist, who
had studied in Germany, Switzerland, France, Italy and
England, had already established his credentials as head
of sales promotion in Wolfsburg's export department.

As a young man, Hahn had admired the creative magic of
Ludwig von Holzschuher, head of advertising at Auto Union
where Hahn's father was in charge of the DKW brand. In the
Third Reich, von Holzschuher was responsible for creating

Carl H. Hahn, the new General Manager of Volkswagen of America.

effective propaganda posters, particularly *Feind hört mit!* ('The enemy is listening!'), warning against potential spies.

"I thus knew about the power of effective advertising,"[5] Hahn says, recalling the agency pitch:

> *"We had looked at about a dozen agencies, the biggest and most beautiful Madison Avenue had to offer. They all made huge presentations in wonderful meeting rooms full of Chairmen of the Board, Executive Vice Presidents, Senior Vice Presidents and Vice Presidents. But we were extremely disappointed. All we saw were Volkswagen ads that looked exactly like every other ad—an airline ad, a cigarette ad, a toothpaste ad. The only difference was that where the tube of toothpaste had been, they had placed a Volkswagen."[6]*

Only one of the agencies that Hahn visited during those first months of 1959 chose not to present speculative ad ideas: DDB. Bill Bernbach was convinced that if a potential client wasn't able to judge the agency from the work it was doing for its current clients, he (or very rarely she) would not be able to judge it all.

Carl H. Hahn:

"Bill Bernbach, Ned Doyle and Maxwell Dane received us in Bernbach's windowless office, with nothing offered but water. Bernbach didn't make any presentation in the proper sense. He just showed us work that DDB had done for other clients and explained to us his way of thinking. I especially liked the ad No Goose No Gander *for El Al and the campaigns for Polaroid and Ohrbach's."*[7]

Hahn's first impression of Bernbach was that of an intelligent, factual, warm-hearted, honest and extremely creative man. "He was no primitive salesman, more of an erudite philosopher with whom you could discuss things really well."[8]

The man who, a couple of weeks earlier, had introduced DDB to Hahn was Arthur Stanton, an important U.S. distributor of Volkswagen who had been looking for an ad agency to promote his New York City dealership Queensboro Motors. It was, in fact, the groundbreaking young photographer Richard Avedon who had told Stanton that DDB was the agency behind the popular Ohrbach's ads.

DDB was invited to develop a concept for the Grand Opening of Queensboro Motors. Stanton liked what was presented and–as a matter of courtesy–asked DDB account supervisor Ed Russell to take the ad to Volkswagen of America and show it to PR chief Scott Stewart and Helmut Schmitz, assistant to advertising manager Paul Lee.

The two Volkswagen men approved the ad, except for one tiny little detail. Ed Russell:

"The second sentence in the ad said something like 'The fender costs only so and so much to replace,' and the third sentence

NO GOOSE

NO GANDER

One of the ads done by DDB that Carl H. Hahn
particularly liked when Bernbach made his agency presentation.

said that service was quick and easy. Schmitz's point was
that [Volkswagen] wanted to put the stress on service, rather
than on replacement parts, and that the third sentence should
therefore come ahead of the second. I disagreed, because I felt
we got the idea across by mentioning the low price of the fender
first and that it was a logical progression from there to go on and
speak about service, once we had established the fact that parts
were inexpensive."[9]

Arthur Stanton–convinced by now that DDB should not only handle the regional Volkswagen advertising, but the national ads, too–invited Russell to meet with him, Paul Lee, Manuel Hinke (VW's export chief) and Carl H. Hahn at the Plaza Hotel in New York City. "Bring that Grand Opening ad along," Stanton told Russell. "I want you to show it to them."[10]

The account supervisor remembered the meeting as follows:

"We had a very nice breakfast and didn't talk about advertising too much, and then, when it came time to go over that ad ... who comes racing in out of breath but Scott Stewart and Helmut Schmitz. They'd heard that this was a breakfast with the ad agency and felt they should be there too. Hahn asked them if they'd seen the ad and Schmitz answered that he had and that he disagreed very strongly with it. That opening remark started the two of us arguing for forty-five minutes ... when we were both almost exhausted, I told the group that I would go back and see what the writer had to say about it. If the writer agreed with the change, then we'd make it. If he didn't, I told him, 'we won't change a line!'"[11]

Russell, it should be mentioned, earned seven battle stars during World War II. "I either blew it or I got it!", he announced to Bernbach after getting back to the agency–he got it.[12]

Later, at a dinner in Wolfsburg, Hahn revealed to the DDB team:

"When we had that breakfast in the Plaza, I'd already seen about four thousand agency people and I had decided that they were all a bunch of phonies. Then, after that breakfast and that argument, I had the feeling I'd finally met an honest man in this business and, if he were honest, he'd give us his best advice."[13]

This great quote is mentioned in Walter Henry Nelson's 1970 book *Small Wonder. The Amazing Story of the Volkswagen*, but it seems Hahn never actually said this. In reality, he had 'only' seen around 120 American ad men and, more importantly, he was too shrewd and professional to choose an agency this way. "Ed Russell was a fabulous account man and became a good friend of mine," says Hahn, "but it would have been a bit childish to pick DDB solely because of his argument

Another ad by DDB that Carl H. Hahn liked, this time for Polaroid.

with Schmitz. We chose DDB because of its outstanding creativity."[14]

In July 1959, the contract between DDB and Volkswagen of America was signed. The advertising budget for the Beetle was a mere $600,000–two percent of what Detroit was prepared to spend for its new 'compacts.'

Volkswagen *really* needed a fantastic advertising campaign.

CHAPTER 4

"Why me? What have I done?"

Julian Koenig and Helmut Krone invent honest advertising

After awarding Doyle Dane Bernbach the Volkswagen account, Carl H. Hahn invited the entire DDB team to Wolfsburg and showed them the VW philosophy at the base. "From the men at the assembly line to the managers. How they functioned. How they lived."[1]

The ad men toured the Volkswagen factory and immersed themselves in the production process of the Beetle. Bill Bernbach remembered days spent talking to engineers, executives and production workers: "We had seen the quality of materials that were used. We had seen

Visiting the Volkswagenwerk in 1959: Helmut Schmitz, Bill Bernbach, Carl H. Hahn and Ned Doyle.

Vance Packard's The Hidden
Persuaders, *from 1957,*
questioned advertising's ethics.

the almost incredible precautions taken to avoid mistakes
… this was an honest car. We had found our selling
proposition."[2]

Bernbach may have simply read Heinz Nordhoff's
statement introducing the 1958 Beetle, though: "In ten short
years the Volkswagen has risen from total obscurity to become
a household name on every continent … Because it does not
pretend to be anything but what it is–an honest car."[3]

As a selling proposition in late-1950s America, honesty
was nothing less than revolutionary. Numerous TV quiz
show scandals had just been uncovered in which popular
contestants were given answers to keep them on the air–
machinations that pharmaceutical and cosmetic sponsors
such as Bristol-Meyers, Geritol and Revlon had apparently
known of and encouraged. The public was shocked, but
hardly surprised, since journalist Vance Packard's book *The
Hidden Persuaders* had already questioned advertising's ethics
and attacked the use of 'Motivational Research' and other
psychology-based techniques to induce desire for products or
approval of politicians. Packard's book, published in 1957 and
topping bestseller lists throughout the year, had a devastating
effect on the image of advertising, with one journalist writing

in 1959: "It is naïve to the point of social ostracism, to believe that advertising can be honest, decent ... and worthy of public belief and trust."[4]

ARGUABLY THE MOST IMPORTANT visitors to Wolfsburg in that summer of 1959 were DDB art director Helmut Krone–34 at the time–and copywriter Julian Koenig, who was 38.

Krone was born in Yorkville, Manhattan's German quarter, after his parents had emigrated from Germany in the mid-1920s. His father, Otto, was a shoemaker, his mother, Emilie, a seamstress. Krone enrolled at the School of Industrial Art in New York City, planning to become a product designer. But the work of Paul Rand, Lester Beall and other hot new graphic talents convinced him that his future lay with print design. Visiting the 1950 New York Art Directors Show–already dominated by DDB after only one year in business–Krone concluded that advertising might also be worth investigating. After stints at *Esquire*, pharmaceutical agency Sudler & Hennessey and fashion agency Diamond Barnett (driving one of the first Beetles imported to the U.S., by the way), Krone joined DDB in 1954. He remembered:

> *"I was 29. Not a kid anymore. I had worked around a lot before then ... I had stayed away from hardcore advertising, however. It's not something you did if you had principles in those days. Instead you took refuge in editorial design for magazines, ads for fashion agencies, annual reports, and pharmaceutical packaging. That was before Bernbach started his agency. When I saw those first ads out of Doyle Dane Bernbach, my eyes popped out of their sockets and I decided advertising could be so good it was worth doing. [Bernbach] changed the face of advertising. He turned it into a profession.*

Helmut Krone originally wanted to become a product designer. But the work of Paul Rand convinced him that his future lay with print design.

You could now go into advertising and tell your mother what you did for a living."[5]

At first following Bob Gage's stripped-down style–large photographs on a white background with big type–Krone quickly developed his own visual philosophy, never settling for second best. DDB folklore has him once wrestling with the label for Thunderbird wine. Stepping into Krone's office, Ned Doyle reminds the art director that DDB resigned that account months ago. "It doesn't matter," Krone replies. "It isn't right yet."[6]

Bob Kuperman–fellow DDB art director and later President and CEO of DDB New York–notes that Krone's perfection wasn't always best for business, though: "He would produce a thousand layouts all of which nobody could tell the difference of. I remember that they put him on a new account called Metrecal, but Helmut took so long to do the work that DDB lost the client."[7]

Krone defended his slowness with wanting to explore all the creative possibilities. He noted:

"Should an ad have a big picture and a small headline?
Or should it have a big headline and a small picture?
Should the logo be a picture?
Or should the picture be a logo?
Should it have six headlines?
Or only one lying on its side?
Should a headline look like the first paragraph of the copy?
Or should it look like the second paragraph of the copy?
Should [the ad] have a picture?
Or should it have half a picture?
Or should it have no picture at all?
The possibilities … are endless."[8]

Julian Koenig, Krone's copy partner on the Volkswagen account, was just as much of a character. Born in 1921 into a New York City family of lawyers and judges, Koenig had studied at Dartmouth and briefly at Columbia Law School before writing an unpublished novel and co-owning a semi-pro baseball team, the Yonkers Indians.

After starting copywriting, Koenig, who considered himself a Marxist, helped to form an advertising union that established, among other things, minimum salaries for copy and art. First he unionized Morton Freund, the small agency he was working at. Later he tried unionizing Grey: "The creatives were all for the Union, the account people and their secretaries against."[9]

At Hirshon Garfield, his next agency, Koenig created one of the most popular campaigns of the 1950s: the Timex 'torture test' commercials with the classic tagline, *Timex: It takes a licking and keeps on ticking.* He then joined the Ellington

Agency where he couldn't get what he considered a good ad through, finally deciding to quit advertising to become a professional gambler.

In 1958, however, after DDB copywriter Rita Selden had told him about an opening, Koenig applied to DDB, "because this was a new form of advertising where copy and art worked together."[10] Even though he was offered "less money than I was making at the track," he took on the job.[11]

One of his first assignments was the aforementioned ad for the Grand Opening of Arthur Stanton's Queensboro Motors dealership, with Helmut Krone as his art partner. The ad wasn't spectacular, but its consequences were: when Bill Bernbach chose the creative team for the new Volkswagen account, he picked the two men already working on it.

KOENIG (MEANING 'KING' in German) and Krone (meaning 'crown') sounded like a perfect match, but as a creative team, they took a while to get used to each other. Julian Koenig:

> "I recall sitting with Helmut for a couple of hours. He was just looking at me and not reacting to any of my thoughts. You know in those days, the person who had the pencil and the pad controlled the ad. That's why I got up and left, saying, 'Helmut, let me know when you're ready.'"[12]

Fellow DDB copywriter David Herzbrun also remembered Krone's difficult character: "When I told a couple of people that I was scheduled to work with Krone, they warned me to prepare for bluntness, rudeness, arrogance, intolerance, cruelty, and stubbornness, and to be prepared to deal with these for a long time."[13] Bob Kuperman agrees: "You would

*Julian Koenig, Helmut Krone's copy partner. Before joining DDB,
he had quit advertising to become a professional gambler.*

quake just to go into Helmut's office. Because you never knew
what to expect."[14]

In the case of the Volkswagen account, though, Krone
might have simply had a problem with selling the 'Führer's
car': "I was wondering what was going on in Bernbach's head.
I didn't think it was something we should do. I said, 'Me? Why
me? What have I done?'"[15]

Although Jewish, Julian Koenig didn't mind promoting the
Beetle. Sure, he proposed showing a picture of Hitler with the
headline, *The man behind the Volkswagen.* But this was just creatively
loosening up. (At the same time, fellow DDBer George Lois made
a flick book where the VW logo became a swastika. "Very funny,
George," Bill Bernbach said. "Now burn it."[16])

"Why should I have had a problem with selling the
Beetle?", Koenig noted:

*"Its first U.S. distributors were all Jews, and by 1959,
Germany and Israel had started getting along, with a lot
of reparations from Germany to Israel. I don't remember
anyone at DDB–nor any of its clients for that matter–having*

*a problem with the account, with the exception of copywriter
David Reider maybe."*[17]

Another reason for Krone's initial refusal to bounce off
Koenig's ideas could have been the honesty approach–a
strategy that didn't convince him at all. "I was dead set against
the Volkswagen campaign as we did it," he said in an interview
from 1968. "I felt that the thing to do with this ugly little car
was to make it as American as possible ... Like, let's get Dinah
Shore also [the best-selling 1940s and '50s singer]. What's that
thing she used to sing? 'See the U.S.A. in your Chevrolet.'
I wanted 'See the U.S.A. in your Volkswagen.' ... I felt so
strongly that we were doing the wrong thing ... that I finished
up three ads, went on vacation to St. Thomas [in the Virgin
Islands], depressed, came back ... and I was a star."[18] Julian
Koenig wasn't aware of this at all. "I never heard a word about
Dinah Shore," he said. "Krone had to be kidding. Anyway,
after a while, our collaboration got better, and rewarding."[19]

One of the consequences of owning a Beetle, account
supervisor Ed Russell discovered, was that its owners often
had to justify the choice of a Volkswagen to others. Why had
they bought such a small car? Why was the engine in the back?
Why was the design always the same? Koenig and Krone
turned the questions on their heads and started to creatively
set forth the specific advantages of owning a Beetle, so that its
owners had more arguments to talk the car up.

The first ad of the campaign, *Is Volkswagen contemplating a
change?*, showing a '59 Beetle next to a '60 model under wraps,
ran in *Life* magazine in late summer 1959 and addressed the
most peculiar feature of the car–its unchanging design. The
second ad, *Why the engine in the back?*, featured the open trunk
and rear-mounted motor of a Beetle and explained the benefits
behind it. The third ad, *Why are people buying Volkswagens faster*

With this sixth Volkswagen ad, from 1959, the "artillery had moved into position and found precise aim," says Clive Challis.

The standard way of doing a car ad in 1959. The Volkswagen campaign couldn't have been more different.

than they can be made?, was a long copy ad, providing eight good arguments for buying a Beetle immediately. The fourth ad, *198 lbs.* (with the subhead, *Why Volkswagen's aluminum engine is still years ahead of its time*), simply showed the motor of the car, reinforcing its compact efficiency. And the fifth ad, *Gerhard Baecker teaches Volkswagen (Or why Volkswagen service is as good as the car)*, featured DDB art director Bill Taubin in front of a chalkboard with a technical drawing of a Beetle, pretending to be instructing VW mechanics.

All these ads roused curiosity in the strange little car, but there was no real graphic consistency as yet. Furthermore, they were rather good advertorials as opposed to great ads. With the sixth ad, however, the "artillery had moved into position and found precise aim," as Helmut Krone biographer Clive Challis writes.[20] The ad showed a lathered Volkswagen, shot from above, with the headline, *The only water a Volkswagen*

Before working with DDB, unrealistic illustrations–mostly done by
Bernd Reuters–had dominated Volkswagen's artwork, too.

needs is the water you wash it with. It was arguably the world's
first advertising headline with a deliberate full stop–now
something no self-respecting copywriter would omit. The
punctuation itself made you stop and wonder how the ad's
copy would justify so much self-confidence.

"Doyle Dane took the exclamation point out of advertising,"
Krone would later say. "I put in the period."[21]

The graphic language for the Volkswagen campaign was
now clearly defined–as honest and basic as the car. The layout
was, at first glance, traditional: two thirds picture, one third
text set in three blocks, with the headline centered in between
the visual and the copy. But the typeface–Futura, created by
the German designer Paul Renner in 1927–was not roman,
as expected in such a classic editorial look. The sans serif
suggested a lack of ornament and pure functionality. As did
the photography: there was no airbrushed illustration of a car,
artificially elongated, with speed lines and little explosions of
light on the hood–just an undoctored, naked Volkswagen.
(Before, this kind of unrealistic artwork had dominated
Volkswagen's brochures, too. The German illustrator Bernd
Reuters had made the Beetle longer and exaggerated the

contours of the wings. He went so far as to reduce the size of the driver to give the illusion of a bigger interior.)

What's more, there was no castle in the background and no glamorous, admiring lady, which was standard at the time. As one American art director remarked: "Car ads are full of broads, mansions, horses, surf, mountains, sunsets, chiseled chins, and caviar–anything but facts."[22]

Carl H. Hahn, however, wanted to treat a human being as a human being, and not as Pavlov's dog. "To me, presenting a car–or any other product for that matter–in such an artificially prestigious way was just plain vulgar. This kind of advertising was degrading America and its great people. They simply deserved better."[23]

Volkswagen's Helmut Schmitz agreed. In a speech to an advertising group in 1963, he said:

> *"It is not Disneyland that people are looking at in our ads. Not a dream world. Not never-never land. It's reality. We just show a car. Sometimes with people. But with real people. Sometimes in a situation. But a real situation … Honesty in advertising requires courage … Requires the courage also to describe what the car is not. What it will not do. What it will not deliver … To be honest in advertising requires the courage to understate rather than overstate."*[24]

The ultimate proof for this understatement was that the Volkswagen ads weren't full color, but black and white–"mainly because we couldn't afford much color," confessed Krone.[25]

All this made for a campaign that shattered contemporary advertising conventions in a way that no campaign had done before–or has done since. ("After VW, everything else is a footnote," says British advertising legend Dave Trott.[26]) Instead of 'too-good-to-be-true,' there was complete honesty. Likewise, Koenig's copy contained no grandiloquent claptrap typical of the car adverts of the day, promising 'turbo thrust' or 'rocket engine action,' just facts, wit and charm. The ads gave the Beetle the personality of the lovable underdog bravely standing up to the bigger, well-established competition with sound arguments such as 'good value for money' or 'high mileage.' You could even argue that by using self-deprecation and irony–traditional elements of Yiddish humor–DDB sold Hitler's car by making it Jewish. (On the other hand, you could rightly ask, as the eminent graphic design writer Steven Heller does, if the strategy to "make the Volkswagen campaign so unapologetic–or shall we say denying–of the Nazi era didn't come straight out of Goebbels' information distortion playbook."[27])

Koenig's copy didn't just *sound* unusual, it also *looked* odd. There were 'orphans' and 'widows' (single words at the beginning or end of a paragraph, and single lines at the top or bottom of a column) that art directors would usually avoid by asking the copywriter to make his text a bit longer or shorter. But Krone "deliberately kept the blocks from being solid ... and when I felt that a sentence could be cut in half I suggested it just to make another paragraph. I wanted the copy to look Gertrude Steiny."[28]

George Lois recalls asking Krone: "Why don't you break the copy so it looks and reads better? Why don't you play with it?"

But Krone said, "No, no, no–when type is set, it's *real,* because a typographer did it, and you should put it down the way he set it. That's honest."

Lois replied, "Are you fucking nuts? I've spent my life cutting type apart, spacing things!"[29]

As Koenig remembered, Bill Bernbach wasn't really involved in those early ads. (But, of course, he had built the only agency in the world where the creative magic of the Volkswagen campaign could happen.)

> *"There never was any formal meeting with Bernbach. I mean, he would walk around the creative department and see the ads we were doing hanging up on Helmut's wall. But we would give the layouts directly to traffic to take them to the account people, who then presented them to the client. The account people may have gone to Bernbach and showed him an ad when they didn't think it was right. But I assume he liked them all because they ran as we did them. The only time Bernbach edited one of my ads was when I had left DDB to start my own agency. I guess this was his reaction to me daring to leave. It was an ad showing a transparent Volkswagen where you could see the interior, including the engine in the back. Bernbach had changed the headline to,* Why are so many people looking into the Volkswagen? *My original headline was,* The least unusual thing about the Volkswagen is the engine in the rear, *which I consider much superior."[30]*

Koenig was happy about someone rewriting another ad of his, though. At its origin was the assignment to make clear that Volkswagens got rejected for the slightest imperfections: a blemished chrome strip on the glove compartment, or a surface scratch barely visible to the eye. In fact, it took over one hundred inspectors to 'okay' a single car, and the head inspector reported to CEO Heinz Nordhoff himself.

Julian Koenig recalled:

> *"One day, my copywriter friend Rita Selden came into Helmut Krone's office and saw a rough of an ad hanging on the wall. It showed a Beetle with the headline,* This Volkswagen missed the boat, *the copy explaining that the 3,389 inspectors in Wolfsburg were saying 'no' to one Volkswagen out of fifty after*

Lemon.

This Volkswagen missed the boat.

The chrome strip on the glove compartment is blemished and must be replaced. Chances are you wouldn't have noticed it; Inspector Kurt Kroner did.

There are 3,389 men at our Wolfsburg factory with only one job: to inspect Volkswagens at each stage of production. (3000 Volkswagens are produced daily; there are more inspectors than cars.)

Every shock absorber is tested (spot checking won't do), every windshield is scanned. VWs have been rejected for surface scratches barely visible to the eye.

Final inspection is really something! VW inspectors run each car off the line onto the Funktionsprüfstand (car test stand), tote up 189 check points, gun ahead to the automatic brake stand, and say "no" to one VW out of fifty.

This preoccupation with detail means the VW lasts longer and requires less maintenance, by and large, than other cars. (It also means a used VW depreciates less than any other car.)

We pluck the lemons; you get the plums.

The revolutionary Lemon *ad from 1960. "We were fully aware how radical the idea was," says Carl H. Hahn.*

final inspection. 'Why don't you write Lemon,*' Rita said. I replied, 'Terrific!', and* This Volkswagen missed the boat *became the first sentence in the body copy."*[31]

The client, however, took more convincing, which didn't surprise Bob Levenson: "Odd in Wolfsburg, odd here, odd everywhere, with no precedent … It was an ad that absolutely flew in the face of convention."[32] Helmut Schmitz was completely against *Lemon*, fearing that many readers would draw negative conclusions. DDB account supervisor Ed Russell–ever the defender of radical creativity–disagreed: "Everyone's going to know that it's a gimmick to induce you to read the ad," he told Schmitz, "VW is not going to spend all those thousands of dollars to say we've got a bad product."[33]

As Schmitz continued to turn down the ad, Russell proposed to do some copy testing. "Go ahead, but we're not going to pay for it," said Volkswagen's advertising manager Paul Lee. Russell shot back: "If the ad fails I'll pay for it–me, personally."[34]

Russell's money was safe. *Lemon* proved to be the most convincing Volkswagen ad ever made. "We were fully aware how radical the idea was," says Carl H. Hahn. Up to this point, advertising had always ignored any potential flaws a product might have. "But since our quality standards were so high, we decided to run the ad."[35] In fact, Hahn was such a great client because of his no-nonsense approach to advertising: why pay for ads if you don't have something relevant to say? If you don't want to get noticed? If you don't want to get talked about? Hahn realized that advertising is an extremely powerful weapon–if you have the guts to use it.

And that's exactly what Volkswagen would continue to do.

CHAPTER 5

"Jesus Christ, that's a great line"

The Volkswagen campaign gets its slogan (almost)

I n the fall of 1959, Volkswagen asked DDB for an ad to appear in a publication from New Jersey's chamber of commerce. It would turn out to be the most revolutionary piece of advertising the world had ever seen–a kind of 'anti-ad' that *Advertising Age* voted the best advertisement of the 20th century.[1]

The brief originally called for a corporate ad in which Volkswagen of America "would talk about how much 'Made in U.S.A.' was used to make the Volkswagen" (such as Pittsburgh steel stamped out on Chicago presses), recalled account supervisor Ed Russell. "Helmut and Julian first came up with a concept that showed Detroit's new Falcon, Corvair and Valiant, headlined *Willkommen* ... I felt ... that it was pushing a little–we were visitors to the United States; imports. And with this high profile we should not get snotty."[2]

Koenig recalled an ad with the headline *Willkommen*, but not an ad showing the first 'compacts' coming out of Detroit:

"I suggested to Helmut an ad with Think small *as the headline, because at that time, American cars were big, America thought big. But Helmut rejected the line, because it was an abstract notion. After a couple of days of arguing, I changed*

The Greek American art director George Lois.

the headline to the German line Willkommen–*in the sense of 'Welcome to the Volkswagen'–and put the words* Think small *in the body copy. The ad, showing a small Beetle, was presented by the account people to Volkswagen in New Jersey. Helmut Schmitz didn't like the line* Willkommen, *which he thought too German. But while reading the body copy, he discovered and liked the words* Think small.*"3*

(If you think that Schmitz would have been a great creative director–so did Bill Bernbach who, in 1966, made him the chief creative of DDB Düsseldorf, the agency's first German subsidiary.)

Yet, Krone still disliked the headline–and refused to finalize the ad. "Julian came to me," remembers George Lois, who was working on the VW Bus at the time, "and said, 'I want to do an ad for Volkswagen, and I can't get Helmut to do it.'" When Koenig told him about his *Think small* idea, Lois responded, "Jesus Christ, that's a great line. You got to convince Krone to do it. You got to *force* him to do it!"4 In Lois' memory, Koenig even wanted him to do a layout. "But I told him, 'Get outta here!'"[5]

It is difficult to know whether Krone's rejection hinged on the headline–or the 'newness' of the idea. He later acknowledged:

"'New' is when you've never seen before what you've just put on a piece of paper. And it's very hard to judge the value of it. You distrust it, and everybody distrusts it. And very often it's somebody else who has to tell you that that thing has merit, because you have no frame of reference, and you can't relate it to anything that you or anybody else has ever done before. Alexey Brodovitch at the New School was the one who put me on to 'new.' Students would bring in something to class that they thought was spectacular, but he'd toss it aside and say: 'I've seen this once before somewhere.' And he wouldn't even discuss it."[6]

Brodovitch, a Russian émigré, was a photographer and designer who art directed the fashion magazine *Harper's Bazaar* from 1934 to 1958. One of the true masters in the world of graphic arts, he worked with innovative photographers such as Man Ray, Henri Cartier-Bresson and Richard Avedon, radically changing American magazine design. The double-page spread was one of his most famous innovations, as was the emphasis on negative space (the space that surrounds an object in an image). "Astonish me!", was Brodovitch's constant challenge to artists and students–an admonition that Helmut Krone would never forget.

"Four or five straight hours with Helmut were more than any writer could take," remembers lauded creative director Marty Cooke. "It was titanically hard work. We weren't just trying to solve the advertising problem at hand;

our mission was nothing less than the reinvention of the art of advertising."[7]

Finally, painfully, after much cajoling, Krone started on layouts for *Think small*, and after several days of figuring out where to put the Beetle on the page, he positioned it in the upper left corner at a slight angle, giving the ad a graphic twist that was as disruptive as Koenig's headline. A couple of weeks later, Krone was laboring on *Think small* again, making the headline smaller and the angle of the car sharper for a consumer version of the original corporate ad to run in magazines such as *Life* and *Look*. And it wasn't just the art that received a tweak: Koenig wrote completely new copy, now targeting potential buyers. He started with the real-life news that "18 New York University students [had] gotten into a sun-roof VW; a tight fit" and ended with: "In 1959 about 120,000 Americans thought small and bought VWs. Think about it."

This first really visible version of *Think small* wasn't met with much enthusiasm by the advertising industry. "The reaction was definitely not, 'This is the ad of the century,'" Julian Koenig recalled. "In fact, I don't remember any particular reaction to *Think small* at all. Only over the years did it become an iconic piece of advertising."[8]

Today, it is almost impossible to perceive just *how* different *Think small* was nearly sixty years ago. Not only did the ad cut through the clutter of the period's car advertising–it cut through the clutter of advertising itself. It was a breakthrough, the start of something completely new. In fact, it was the advertising equivalent to the numerous artistic transformations that took place at the very same time.

In 1959, the saxophonist Ornette Coleman released *The Shape of Jazz to Come*, a pivotal album in the genesis of avant-garde music. The cylindrical design of the new Guggenheim

"Jesus Christ, that's a great line"

Think small.

18 New York University students have gotten into a sun-roof VW; a tight fit. The Volkswagen is sensibly sized for a family. Mother, father, and three growing kids suit it nicely.

In economy runs, the VW averages close to 50 miles per gallon. You won't do near that; after all, professional drivers have canny trade secrets. (Want to know some? Write VW,

Box #65, Englewood, N. J.) Use regular gas and forget about oil between changes.

The VW is 4 feet shorter than a conventional car (yet has as much leg room up front). While other cars are doomed to roam the crowded streets, you park in tiny places.

VW spare parts are inexpensive. A new front fender (at an authorized VW dealer) is

$21.75.* A cylinder head, $19.95.* The nice thing is, they're seldom needed.

A new Volkswagen sedan is $1,565.* Other than a radio and side view mirror, that includes everything you'll really need.

In 1959 about 120,000 Americans thought small and bought VWs. Think about it.

The first consumer version of Think small *from 1959. Today, it is almost impossible to perceive just how different the ad was nearly sixty years ago.*

museum by Frank Lloyd Wright polarized critics, and yet went on to become a landmark work of 20th-century architecture. The so-called 'pop artists'–such as Jasper Johns, Claes Oldenburg or Robert Rauschenberg–had their first shows, challenging the public by employing objects and images of mass culture, from comic books to news and advertising. The world of cinema was undergoing a transformation, too, as John Cassavetes' movie *Shadows* proved, also released in 1959. Not only was its plot around an interracial relationship deeply disturbing to the general public–Hollywood became nervous because Cassavetes had raised the money for the production of the movie from friends and family, and even from the listeners of a late-night radio talk-show. (An early form of crowdsourcing that proved that there was an alternative to the studio production system.) All the while, author Joseph Heller was writing *Catch-22*, a satirical novel set during World War II–a "wild, moving, shocking, hilarious, raging, exhilarating, giant roller-coaster of a book," as the *Herald Tribune* commented.[9] Another example of how things were changing was the comedy of Lenny Bruce "who uncorked elaborate monologues about sex, drugs, religion and politics," as cultural historian Fred Kaplan observes.[10] Nobody had ever laughed at jokes like this before.

Thus, it wasn't just the Volkswagen campaign that broke with the conventions of the time, but it did this just as radically and skillfully, and in particular with *Think small*: the little Beetle, almost as small as a postage stamp, was placed against a background of stark white nothingness. The only other tiny visual, the Volkswagen logo, was oddly placed, too–not bottom right to sign off the ad, but left aligned in the third column. (Krone initially wanted to show an actual Volkswagen car key in his ads, but the key's shape kept changing, so he dropped the idea.) Finally, there was the almost heretical imperative of

Think small, which could have served as a slogan (or strapline) for the entire Volkswagen campaign, but Bernbach didn't like slogans, since advertising was–and still is–full of them.

Marketing legend Al Ries, co-author of the seminal book *Positioning: The Battle for Your Mind*, compared 146 car ads from the 1950s with *Think small*. Almost all of them, Ries noted, included people: "How else was a creative director going to demonstrate the pleasure that car buyers might feel about their new acquisitions?" Almost all used artwork as opposed to photography, in order to make the cars look long and low and beautiful. Most used illustrations to communicate all of the car's exciting features. Comparison of these adverts with *Think small* is "the difference between complexity and simplicity. Between artificiality and realism."[11]

It was also the difference between going broke and continuing a success story. Within twenty-four months of the launch of the first American-made small cars, the U.S. sales of imported cars–most of them 'compacts'–fell from 614,000 in 1959 to 379,000 in 1961. Only VW sales were unaffected. In fact, registrations of Beetles even rose, reaching 150,000 in 1961. "And while Detroit had to grant huge discounts to get rid of its cars," Carl H. Hahn chuckles, "Volkswagen could raise the price of the Beetle every year."[12] Thinking small paid off big.

"That's the whole fun in creativity, isn't it?", says Dave Trott: "How to make the underdog beat the top dog. How to use creativity as a legal unfair advantage, as Ed McCabe [a legendary copywriter] put it."[13]

In fact, the Volkswagen campaign could constitute another chapter in *David and Goliath*, Malcolm Gladwell's best-selling book from 2013 about the *Art of Battling Giants*: Goliath was Detroit, the Volkswagen was David–and DDB's creativity was his sling.

CHAPTER 6

"Cross off 'Dear Charlie'"

Bob Levenson perfects the campaign's tone of voice

When Julian Koenig left DDB at the end of 1959 to start his own agency, Bernbach decided that David Reider–DDB's copy chief–should be the new writer on Volkswagen. Helmut Krone and Reider, however, couldn't stand being in the same room together. Bob Levenson noted that there was "bad chemistry between the two of them. Maybe because Reider was an old school guy who wouldn't let an art director tell him how long his copy should be."[1] Or maybe Reider was upset by Krone's notoriously bad mood. The art director claimed that he had a good reason for it, though. He noted:

> *"As children we're taught to obey rules. If you're being creative you are breaking rules. A basic desire to be well-liked is a serious problem if you want to be creative … You can't be nice and answer the assignment in a radically new way. Because you're going to throw out some of the rules in the process. And throwing out some of the rules is not the 'nice' thing to do. It doesn't make you popular with your peers."[2]*

After the summer of 1960, things had become so strained that Reider asked Bob Levenson to take over. Levenson, then 31, had been working in DDB's sales promotion department,

Bob Levenson, Helmut Krone's third copy partner.

shortening Koenig's and Reider's VW copy to fit smaller formats. "I knew something about *cutting* copy, not *writing* copy," Levenson remembered.

> "So when Reider came into my office and asked me how I was doing, I said, 'David, I can't do this.' Reider took my hand—with the pencil in it—in his hand and actually wrote out the first sentence of the body copy for me: 'Here's a side of the Volkswagen that very few people know about: the underside.' Then he said, 'Now you can do it.' And I did."[3]

After this hesitant start, Krone and Levenson quickly became one of the most prolific creative teams on the Volkswagen account ever, producing classics such as *The '51 '52 '53 '54 '55 '56 '57 '58 '59 '60 '61 Volkswagen* or *No point showing the '62 Volkswagen. It still looks the same*, probably the first ad ever to employ no visual as its visual.

One might expect the idea of buying expensive advertising space without even showing the car to have raised some eyebrows in Wolfsburg. Carl H. Hahn, however, confirms that Volkswagen recognized the radical ad for what is was— pure genius. "The ad was unique, that's true. But so was our car. With its unchanging design and our utter contempt of planned obsolescence, the Volkswagen was in every respect

Krone and Levenson were one of the most prolific VW teams ever, producing classics such as this one.

Done in 1961, this is probably the first ad in advertising history to employ no visual as its visual.

the opposite of Detroit. And not showing our new model in an ad was a great way to prove this."[4]

Bob Levenson may not have created the tone of voice of the Volkswagen campaign, but he certainly perfected it. Krone observed that the copywriter was the first to understand "that the VW ads' special graphic form required a new way of copy. Shorter, faster, more efficient, yet with the car's personality."[5] Bernbach would later refer to Levenson's copy style as "subject, verb, object."[6]

Dave Trott knows how it came about:

"When Helmut Krone was designing the look of the Volkswagen campaign. Julian Koenig's copy was just a big block, and Krone thought, 'This is impenetrable, this is too hard to read.' So he got his scalpel and started cutting windows into the copy. The next day, Koenig came in and Krone said to

The 1960 rework of Think small *became DDB's official version of the ad.*

> *him, 'Can you re-write the copy like this?' Koenig said, 'Well, I can, but some of the sentences will be only one word long, and that's not grammatical.' Krone said, 'It doesn't matter. It looks good, it looks accessible, it looks readable.'"[7]*

In the fall of 1960, Krone and Levenson decided to rework the existing consumer version of *Think small*. With its even smaller headline and even sharper angle of the car, this third version of the ad–complete with new copy–became the one that the agency would use for self-promotion. Yet, Levenson maintained, it was never a favorite of Krone's, despite including *Think small* in a 1984 exhibition of his work at the Art Center College of Design in Pasadena, California. Maybe Krone's problem was that the ad breaks a fundamental rule of creative advertising: don't show what you say, and don't say what you show. *Think small* is a great, provocative line, but in combination with the visual of a small car, it doesn't create maximum visual-verbal synergy. ("I suppose you want to make the car small?", Krone said without enthusiasm when Koenig showed him his *Think small* line.[8])

Levenson disagreed with this argument: "A big car with *Think small* or a small car with *Think big* just wouldn't work. You have to remember the way we felt about rules. If there is a rule, we said, let's break it."[9] With one exception, Levenson famously insisted:

> *"When you really don't know what to put on that blank paper in the typewriter, you should just write 'Dear Charlie' at the top. Assume that Charlie is a neighbor of yours, a very nice, bright, intelligent guy, with a sense of humor. He's got all the mental equipment you have, but none of the information that you have about the Volkswagen. So just put down what you want to tell him in this ad, and cross off 'Dear Charlie,' and you'll probably be all right."[10]*

For Bob Levenson, this simple creative philosophy worked– he is considered the 'writer's writer,' the best print copywriter ever. But for many, the finest piece of writing he ever did was when Bill Bernbach had died from leukemia in 1982. "I've written about Bill before," Levenson said in front of the mourners. "More than once or twice. And when I showed him what I had written, I was happy that he never changed a word. Now I would be even happier if he could change them all. Goodbye, my friend."[11]

Helmut Krone also bid farewell to Bernbach:

> *"We would have had one of our little disagreements with the ad that ran today [Bernbach's obituary]. I had wanted it to say 'William Bernbach' instead of 'Bill.' I can see [his] face now. I show him the ad with 'William' in it and he nods approval, but it's definitely not a ten.*

Bill Bernbach
1911-1982

He said,
"The real giants have always been poets,
men who jumped from facts
into the realm of imagination and ideas."

He elevated advertising to high art
and our jobs to a profession.

He made a difference.

DDB's obituary ad for Bill Bernbach.

So I say, 'Is there something that disturbs you about it—like the first line, maybe? How do you like William, *Bill?'*

'I'm not crazy about it, Helmut.'

'Bill, let me explain something about typography. It looks better if you start it with a slightly longer line.'

And he says, 'Helmut, what did you just call me?'

And I say, 'Bill.'

And he says, 'Right, so make it Bill.'"[12]

"We did it to see Bill's eyes light up,"[13] Bob Gage once said about the creative spirit at DDB.

CHAPTER 7

"Will we ever kill the bug?"

Len Sirowitz gives the Volkswagen ads a new twist

Only three years after its start, the Volkswagen campaign was already considered a classic–which made Len Sirowitz' job even harder. The art director had joined DDB at the end of 1959 at the age of 27, after stints at pharmaceutical agency L.W. Froelich, Grey, CBS Television Network and Channel Thirteen. In 1962, he started working on Volkswagen as the first art director to succeed Helmut Krone whom Bernbach wanted on other assignments. "What an act to follow," Sirowitz remembers. "It was scary as hell."[1]

Volkswagen CEO Heinz Nordhoff once said that his greatest achievement was resisting the urge to change the Beetle's original design. Sirowitz says something similar about the look of the Volkswagen campaign: "I thought it was brilliant. Simple and very refreshing. That's why I wanted to stay with it. What's more, was I to come into the account and foolishly make changes? Change for the sake of change? Prove my individuality at the expense of VW and the agency? No, that would have been wrong."[2]

And yet, Sirowitz was faced with a major challenge. He did not want to change the look of the campaign, but, as a

Len Sirowitz, the first art director to succeed Helmut Krone on Volkswagen. "What an act to follow," he remembers. "It was scary as hell."

creative person, he did not want to simply copy Helmut Krone, either–he wanted to infuse the campaign with his own style and humor. And he succeeded, as the 1965 ad *Will we ever kill the bug?* proves.

In what was to become an unforgettable shoot, a brand new VW was borrowed from a local dealer and suspended from a huge crane so that it could be gently lowered and set down on its roof (like a dead bug). Sirowitz remembers:

> *"The late afternoon light was beautiful. The photographer, with his camera on a tripod in a locked in position, was ready to shoot. And then it happened: in a split second after the car touched the ground, its roof collapsed. Fortunately, the camera had already clicked off two shots, before we had to get up the nerve to return the damaged car to a very unhappy Volkswagen dealer."[3]*

Another iconic Beetle ad by Sirowitz was *Green Fender*, also from 1965, showing a multi-colored Beetle composed of parts from older models. For this ad, Sirowitz–in spite of the awe

A VW ad done by Sirowitz in 1965. "The camera had
clicked off two shots when the roof collapsed," he remembers.

for his predecessor—chose to completely abandon Krone's classic look. There was no headline, and not even a logo, since Sirowitz managed to convince Volkswagen that it would only get in the way. Krone must have loved the ad when he saw it. "I've spent my whole life fighting logos," he said in an interview from 1979. "Logos say 'I am an ad. Turn the page.'"[4] It might well have been the radicalness of this ad that prompted the creative commentator of *Advertising Age* to write in 1965:

> *"VW advertising is so much in a class by itself, that it has almost removed itself from consideration by people in advertising. By that I mean that whereas all other advertising is considered in a frame of competitive reference, Volkswagen's is not. It stands alone and thus beyond critical comparisons."*[5]

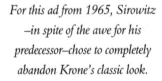

For this ad from 1965, Sirowitz –in spite of the awe for his predecessor–chose to completely abandon Krone's classic look.	*A master class in consumer psychology (and the inspiration for this book's title): the ad* Ugly is only skin-deep *from 1965.*

What made this compliment even more flattering was the fact that by the mid-1960s, the Creative Revolution in advertising was in full swing. Inspired by the success of DDB, a slew of other creative agencies were thriving, although Bill Bernbach, at first, didn't think this possible. George Lois–who, with Papert Koenig Lois, set up the first creative agency outside of DDB on January 1, 1960–remembers telling Bernbach that he and Julian Koenig were leaving:

> "We had walked into Bill's office, wearing jackets and with no ads in our hands, which must have been a hell of a signal to him that something was wrong here. 'Look, Bill,' I said. 'We are not taking any accounts with us. We are going with nothing– nothing but our talent.' Bill replied, 'You got to understand: there can't be more than one creative agency in the world.'"[6]

65

The "maestro," as Lois respectfully called Bernbach, was wrong. The huge success of Papert Koenig Lois proved that great advertising was possible without his help and inspired dozens of creatives to start their own agency, such as Leber Katz Paccione, who suggested, *If you run out of Löwenbräu ... order champagne*; Carl Ally, who told the prospective buyers of a Volvo to *Drive it like you hate it*; Wells, Rich, Greene, who declared on behalf of Braniff International Airlines *The end of the plain plane*; or Scali, McCabe, Sloves, who made Frank Perdue from Perdue Farms a household name with their campaign, *It takes a tough man to make a tender chicken.*

The success of these new creative boutiques was a direct result of the dramatic social change that had been taking place in the U.S. since the 1950s. Due to the economic boom, there was increasing affluence, particularly among the huge numbers of young Americans born after World War II–the so-called 'Baby Boomers.' Convinced that their generation was profoundly different from the one before, a lot of the Boomers rejected the values of their parents and had their own fashion (e.g. blue jeans), music (most notably rock 'n' roll), slang ('cool' and 'neat'), movies (such as *The Wild One* with Marlon Brando), and moral views (particularly since the launch of the Pill).

Until the early 1960s, "the big agencies on Madison Avenue were either unaware of these changes, or unconcerned by them," notes Alfredo Marcantonio who is a Baby Boomer himself.[7] In fact, the traditional agencies' "upright Harvard and Yale graduates were increasingly out of touch with the people they were trying to influence,"[8] he says, continuing to produce the kind of old school lecture type advertising that a new generation of more liberal, hedonistic and diverse Americans had grown tired of.

The 'ethnics' in the new creative agencies, however, were able to decipher what was going on, sympathizing with the

Bob Levenson and Helmut Krone had succeeded in making the Beetle an American icon, as with this ad from 1962.

By 1963, the Beetle was on the way to becoming the new Ford Model T, which this ad expressed (albeit with a Model A).

'rebels without a cause,' and speaking the idiom of the times. "All of a sudden, it was the streetwise, not the book-wise, who knew how to communicate and capture people's imagination," observes Marcantonio.[9] And with seventy-six million Americans born between 1945 and 1964, knowing how to talk to them was, of course, a huge economic advantage. In fact, advertisers increasingly shifted their budgets from old school Madison Avenue agencies to the new creative boutiques.

Despite of the success of the Creative Revolution that it helped trigger, DDB's Volkswagen campaign continued to

That's how many times we inspect a Volkswagen.

It makes your house look bigger.

Same proposition as in the Lemon *ad*
three years earlier, but different idea.

Another ad showing—like
Think small—*a tiny little Beetle.*

define the gold standard of smart creativity. Such as with the ad *Ugly is only skin-deep*, produced by Len Sirowitz in 1965. It delivers a master class in consumer psychology, for, essentially, products are like people—we like them more when they're able to make a joke about themselves or when they admit their flaws. By acknowledging the disadvantages of the car you're trying to sell, a prospective customer will trust you far more. In fact, studies have shown that if a salesperson tries extra hard to fight someone's resistance, that person will become defensive. The solution is to take advantage of the concerns that a prospect may have with your product. Agree with his doubts, then find a way to overcome them. *Yes, you're right: the Volkswagen is homely. It is small and noisy. But it has a lot of personality—like you do, too, don't you? And it is economical, reliable and very well made.*

The *Ugly* ad does exactly that and this way turns a weakness into a strength. The artful admission of a disadvantage makes the advantages of the Volkswagen all the more believable.

Sirowitz–another Jew working on the account–was sometimes uncomfortable selling Hitler's car, but the amazing job that Bob Levenson and Helmut Krone had done in making the Beetle an American icon–such as in the ad with a Volkswagen next to a Coke bottle and the line, *2 shapes known the world over*–helped him overcome the issue. It wasn't always easy to put it aside, though, especially during visits to Wolfsburg.

Sirowitz chuckingly tells of an orientation trip to the Volkswagen factory with Bob Levenson:

> *"So there we were, two Jewish boys, in a restaurant in Braunschweig, having dinner with Volkswagen executives who had probably served in Hitler's Wehrmacht. We were drinking away when all of a sudden, one of the Volkswagen guys started lamenting the sad economic state that Germany was in and concluded, 'If only we hadn't lost those two wars– we'd be better off!' Bob and I started looking at each other, Bob turning redder and redder, until he told the guy, 'That's right– you lost two in a row!' The tension mounted. But fortunately, that guy's boss put his arm around him and said, 'Hans, I think you just lost a third!'"*[10]

George Lois feels that Bill Bernbach (who was Jewish) also had a problem with selling the 'Führer's car.' He claims: "Bill told me that he only wanted to keep Volkswagen for a year or so, to prove that DDB could create truly great car advertising, too, and land the giant GM car account."[11]

"Nonsense," said Julian Koenig, though, when confronted with Lois' statement: "It was one of Bernbach's principles that the agency would never dump an account in order to take on a bigger rival. Although I must admit that shortly after I left DDB for Papert Koenig Lois, Bernbach dumped Schenley's to take on Seagram's, another liquor account."[12]

With ads like this one from 1965, Bob Levenson became the 'writer's writer.'

"Julian is right," remembered Bob Levenson. "But we didn't take on Seagram's because it was a bigger account. Lewis Rosenstiel, the President of Schenley's, was a prick who didn't have any respect for us and the other advertising agencies working for him. So when the opportunity came along to get Seagram's, DDB dumped Schenley's."[13]

Yet, George Lois insists on remembering Bill Bernbach's initial strategy: "When Volkswagen started to become a big account, I told Bill, 'Thank God you are so successful with it. Who wants to work on fucking GM cars?' Because that's what he wanted. He was going for GM!"[14]

Whatever the case may be, DDB was doing extremely well by the mid-1960s, even without GM, handling a slew of major national accounts: Bristol-Myers, Gillette, Heinz, Lever Brothers, Mobil Oil, Seagram, Sony, UniRoyal, or United Airlines.

"Will we ever kill the bug?"

**They said it couldn't be done.
It couldn't.**

*An ad from 1966. "Honesty in advertising requires the courage to understate
rather than overstate," remarked VW's Helmut Schmitz.*

As a special badge of honor, John F. Kennedy had approached
DDB for help with his re-election campaign. After the tragic
death of JFK, Vice President Lyndon B. Johnson continued the
collaboration, resulting in the production of the TV commercial
Daisy for the 1964 election. Though it only aired once, the
ad is considered a major factor in Johnson's landslide victory
over Barry Goldwater whom the commercial accused of being
willing to start a nuclear war against the Soviets.

With total billings of $174 million in 1965, DDB moved
into the ranks of the top players. What's more, the agency
created subsidiaries outside the U.S. wherever Volkswagen
asked it to, the first office opening in Düsseldorf, Germany,
in 1962. "We globalized DDB long before that term was
coined,"[15] says Carl H. Hahn who, in recognition of his
achievements, was called back to Wolfsburg in 1964 to join

the Volkswagen Executive Board and eventually became CEO of the Volkswagen Group in 1982.

In charge of setting up the German branch were copywriter David Herzbrun and art director Paul Wollman who were sent over from the New York City office. But it was Sirowitz and Levenson who remained responsible for the VW account, the two of them supervising many other writers and art directors.

Together, they produced at least thirty or more ads each year. All of them were just like those created by Julian Koenig and Helmut Krone before. They were simple, different–and honest. "Just say as skillfully as you can … what it really is that you are selling, what is good about it and why somebody should buy it instead of what they are buying now," Levenson demanded of his creative teams.[16]

And there was something else that made the VW campaign unique. In a book about the psychology of breakthroughs, business consultants Mark Barden and Adam Morgan coined the term 'a beautiful constraint.' The reasoning behind it: a constraint is generally seen as a "limitation, imposed by outside circumstances or by ourselves, that materially affects our ability to do something."[17] That's why most of us tend to see constraints as adversely limiting. But, in fact, the opposite is true: constraints must not be restrictive, they can be "fertile forces of enhancement, stimulating new possibilities,"[18] as Barden and Morgan put it.

The Volkswagen campaign demonstrates this perfectly. It uses a constraint–the lack of sufficient advertising dollars–as a stimulus to create a completely new advertising approach. If you want to persuade people, DDB and Volkswagen realized, the currency is not money. Instead, it's the ability to connect through great ideas. In fact, DDB's Volkswagen ads did exactly what the oddly shaped car did: they made people talk.

And with the extension of the campaign to another medium, DDB was given the chance to make them talk even more.

CHAPTER 8

"Intelligent irreverence"

Roy Grace and John Noble televise the advertising revolution

Attracting attention and maintaining it with a strong selling point–DDB had been master of the art of print advertising for well over a decade now, but the agency's TV commercials were not yet at the same level. In 60 seconds (the average length of a TV spot in the 1960s), the viewer had to be involved in a compelling story and hit with a surprising ending.

DDB's first attempts to bring Volkswagen to television were somewhat awkward, in part, perhaps, because while Helmut Krone may have been the best print art director ever, his talents did not translate quite so brilliantly to the small screen.

The TV adaptation of *Think small* from 1960 begins by literally reproducing the print ad, but without the Beetle and the VW logo.

"This year," a voiceover announces, "just about everyone's coming up with a brand new small car. So this year, just about everyone will be telling you about this great new idea–to *think small*. It *is* a great idea," the voice-over continues as a real Beetle is being driven to the upper left corner of the print ad and two engineers place a big VW logo between the second and the third column of the copy: "We at Volkswagen have been working on it for 21 years."

As Len Sirowitz moved on to produce another legendary campaign (for Mobil), Roy Grace became head art director on VW in 1965.

This ad was undoubtedly clever, self-referential and highly conceptual (watch it on tinyurl.com/ugly-think), but, essentially, a print ad in motion.

Three years later, copywriter David Herzbrun and art director Paul Wollman from DDB Düsseldorf set out to crack the TV code. The creative team had just produced another milestone print ad for the Beetle: *Some shapes are hard to improve on* showed the back of a Volkswagen drawn in black marker on an egg–a textbook example of the seamless integration of a straightforward line and a strong visual that is the *sine qua non* of creative advertising.

Hot on the heels of this success, Herzbrun and Wollman came up with a TV commercial that starts with a Beetle traveling on a snow-covered untracked country road at the break of dawn. In scene after scene, the car's headlights illuminate the heavy drifts of fresh snow, piling up higher and higher on the winding, climbing road that the Beetle easily surges through. No music is heard. The only sound is the intrepid purr of the engine. The suspense is mounting: who is the driver, and where is he heading to? Finally, the Beetle

David Herzbrun and Paul Wollman produced this great ad.

arrives at a large dark building, and the driver gets out of the car. Then, in a big garage, headlights go on, a powerful engine comes to life, and a huge snow plow rolls past, leaving the snow-covered Beetle alone on screen.

Shot in the canton of Vaud in Switzerland, the commercial took several days to film. There "was not a road that hadn't been perfectly plowed all winter long," remembered David Herzbrun.

> *"We created our own roads by driving the car parallel to lines of utility poles that crossed open fields. Each location we found could only be used for one take, because each called for trackless roads. We moved our cars and crew throughout the district, shooting for a full week, shivering in the icy fog."[1]*

The pain was worth it: the Museum of Modern Art in New York selected the spot as the first TV commercial to be included

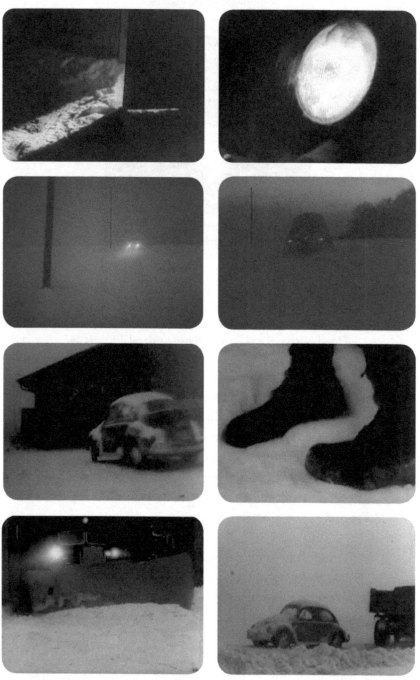

Shot in Switzerland, Snow Plow, *from 1963, was voted the 'Best Television Commercial of the Century.' Watch it on tinyurl.com/ugly-snowplow*

in their permanent film collection, and in 1999, *Snow Plow* was voted the 'Best Television Commercial of the Century' at the Cannes Lions International Festival of Creativity. Herzbrun and Wollman had to share the credit with Bob Levenson and Len Sirowitz, though, who reworked the commercial to adapt it for the U.S. market.

"The original voice-over in German went on and on and never got to the point," Sirowitz remembers:

"So Bob and I wrote an entirely new copy, just a few lines dispersed throughout the commercial, including the now famous question, 'Have you ever wondered how the man who drives a snow plow drives to the snow plow? This one drives a Volkswagen. So you can stop wondering.'"[2]

SNOW PLOW IS A BRILLIANT idea but Volkswagen's finest minutes in television were still to come, as art director Roy Grace and copywriter John Noble set out to prove.

Grace joined DDB New York in 1964, at the age of 28, with stints at Benton & Bowles, Grey and DDB Düsseldorf before. As Sirowitz moved on to produce another legendary campaign (*We want you to live* for Mobil)–an account that DDB snatched up from Rosser Reeves' stumbling agency Ted Bates– Grace became head art director on the Volkswagen account in 1965. "An extremely competitive person," remembers Bob Kuperman. "Roy could be very sarcastic and hard on those who lacked talent. He had a great sense of humor, though, and was very sharp regarding getting to concept."[3]

That same year, John Noble started copywriting on VW, becoming head copywriter in 1966. "When I was asked to work on the Volkswagen account," he remembered, "my hands were sweaty and … my collar was too tight." He had "the feeling that all the great Volkswagen ads had already been done."[4]

Fortunately, they hadn't, not only in print, but also in television where Grace and Noble managed to make the Beetle just as lovable. *Keeping up with the Kremplers* from 1967 is one of their most memorable commercials.

The spot opens on two neighbors, Mr. Jones and Mr. Krempler, who each have $3,000 to spend. With his money, Mr. Jones goes out and buys himself a new Ford. Mr. Krempler, however, buys himself a new refrigerator, a new range, a new washer, a new dryer, a record player, two new television sets—and a brand new Volkswagen. All for the same $3,000. "Now Mr. Jones is faced with that age-old problem," the announcer drily comments: "Keeping up with the Kremplers."

In 1969, Grace and Noble produced another classic by, once more, defying the rules of traditional advertising.

"We owed the client two commercials," remembered Grace, but they hadn't had any ideas that they deemed worthy.[5] After a weekend at his vacation home in Woodstock, Grace was driving back to New York City when he encountered a funeral cortege coming the other way.

"I often would try and work on the drive back, just sort of free-associate with things,"[6] he recalled:

> *"I thought that a funeral would be the last thing on which you would base an ad. But then I thought, why not? It was relevant. It was full of cars. It was also wrong and irreverent, which was, of course, the point. But it had to be intelligent irreverence, and completely tie into the values we had established for the brand."[7]*

By the time Grace arrived in the city, he had developed a TV idea around a thrifty billionaire who bequeaths all of his riches

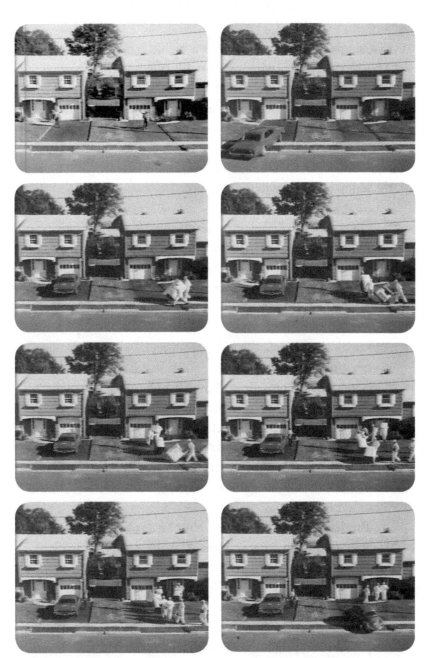

With Keeping up with the Kremplers *from 1967, Roy Grace and copywriter John Noble managed to make the Beetle as lovable in TV as it had been in print. Watch it on tinyurl.com/ugly-kremplers*

to a single person: the driver of a highly economical Beetle. This is what Grace, who would eventually become Chairman and Chief Creative Officer of DDB U.S. in 1982, meant by 'intelligent irreverence': in much of TV advertising–then as well as now–the entertainment is merely *added* to the sales proposition as a trick to lure the viewer into watching the commercial. Grace's funeral idea, however, inextricably links the entertainment with the product.

> *"Here's the test,"* said Bob Levenson: *"If you look at a commercial and fall in love with the brilliance of it, try taking the product out of it. If you still love the commercial, it's no good. Don't make your commercial interesting; make your product interesting."[8]*

And that's exactly what Roy Grace's funeral idea did. In fact, the art director got so excited about it that he, at first, didn't have "the guts to present it to the client because I thought it was too controversial. You don't fool around with funerals. Nor did I know that the client's brother had just died and he had gone to the funeral that previous week. But the client bought it. And that's the difference in the world today. You didn't have to sell those things," Grace said, Volkswagen just "bought them."[9]

But having a client approve your idea is only the starting point of producing a great commercial. After the hard work of coming up with a brilliant storyboard, the even harder work of bringing it to life begins. What helps is picking the right director. For *Funeral*, Roy Grace chose Howard Zieff who was a great photographer as well, notably for DDB's most socially progressive campaign to date: *You don't have to be Jewish to love Levy's*, featuring a large variety of ethnically diverse people, all enjoying Levy's rye bread.

DDB's most socially progressive campaign to date, featuring a large variety of ethnically diverse people, all enjoying Levy's rye bread.

"What a great campaign," remembers Dave Trott who was working in New York City at the time:

> *"What was clearly wrong in those days was that anyone in advertising was represented as White Anglo-Saxon Protestant. Bill Bernbach began putting Jews and Blacks, Irish and Italians in his ads, celebrating the differences instead of pretending they didn't exist. That's the power of advertising. It can be a force for good."*[10]

The *Funeral* spot starts with a never-ending convoy of large luxury cars in a funeral cortege. As the voice of the deceased announces the will, we see various wasteful mourners–all wonderfully cast–looking forward to benefitting from his riches: his wife Rose, his sons Rodney and Victor, his business partner Jules. But only his nephew Harold, driving a modest

*Attention-grabbing, warm, funny and yet clearly focused on the product:
the TV commercial* Funeral *from 1969. Watch it on tinyurl.com/ugly-funeral*

black Beetle at the end of the convoy and wiping away a tear, inherits the departed's entire fortune of 100 billion dollars.

Attention-grabbing, warm, funny and yet clearly focused on the product–with *Funeral*, DDB had creatively developed to define the gold standard for TV advertising, too. With this ad, as well as with a slew of others before, Volkswagen redefined the criteria of choice in the automotive category in its favor. While Detroit kept tapping into the allegedly American ideas of power, speed and luxury, VW emphasized another set of American values: frugality, simplicity, durability.

In a funny way, the Volkswagen campaign did exactly what Helmut Krone had originally wanted to do–it Americanized the German car, but by another route. The Volkswagen was the car for the Americans who knew better than Detroit–and who were proud of it. So proud, in fact, that they became the Beetle's best salesmen, completely embracing the VW philosophy and remaining loyal to the brand for years.

These true believers–or 'brand evangelists,' as marketers would call them today–formed a "fast growing church of motoring missionaries that sang the praises of their purchase far and wide," as Alfredo Marcantonio puts it.[11] Some Volkswagen owners even mimicked the campaign's irreverent tone of voice when they advertised their used Beetle: "Must sell 2 boys or Volkswagen. Your choice, $926.26."[12]

(Concerning the recent emissions scandal, eminent advertising commentator Bob Hoffman notes that if Volkswagen "recover (and they will) the essential element to their recovery will be the reservoir of positive sentiment their advertising has created among consumers."[13])

And yet, the *Funeral* commercial was an omen. A reminder that all things must pass.

Even the world's greatest ad campaign.

CHAPTER 9

"It took me a year to sell that ad"

Bob Kuperman keeps the campaign great until the end

As VW dealers found prospects often stepping into their showroom with the headline of the latest DDB ad on their lips, Volkswagen's sales grew steadily, and not just in the U.S. By 1968, the Beetle had become the best-selling car in the world. In America alone, there were almost a thousand dealerships. In an eerie way, Hitler's dream had come true: the Volkswagen was the People's Car. Maybe to VW's detriment, too, says Ed McCabe: "By tying the company to the fun little Beetle so strongly, it became nearly impossible for Volkswagen to market larger more serious cars. The Beetle campaign put VW into a 30-year marketing hole."[1]

As Wolfsburg produced more and more cars, DDB produced more and more ads, and their quality was kept high. Substantially responsible for this was Bob Kuperman who joined the agency in 1963, at the age of 22, fresh out of art school. The young art director had almost passed on the opportunity to join the Hogwarts of advertising creativity. When DDB Vice President Ben Spiegel called Kuperman on a Friday afternoon asking him to join, Bob refused, since the proposed $65-a-week salary was less than the $85-a-week he was currently making. "I told Ben that I wanted to take the weekend to think it over," recalls Kuperman. "He said, 'Do

Bob Kuperman started working on Volkswagen in 1967
and succeeded Roy Grace as head art director shortly after.

you realize that there's a line out the door to work here?' So I said, 'Well, if you can't give me the weekend, give the job to the next guy in line.'"[2]

In 1967, after a couple of years on other accounts, Kuperman started working on Volkswagen and succeeded Roy Grace as creative supervisor on VW in 1969. Like Grace and Sirowitz, Kuperman never considered changing the look of the campaign. "Of course not," he remembers:

> *"It was considered the bible, and rightly so. Helmut Krone had said a great thing–that he was trying to create a page for every account he was working on. And he definitely achieved this with Volkswagen. Even if you didn't really look at the ads, you knew from thirty feet away that they were for the Beetle. That was Helmut's genius. To see a page as a canvas."[3]*

But in spite of his awe for Krone's classic look, Kuperman was ready to break new graphic ground if this helped express his

This Kuperman ad from 1971 is considered one of the campaign's best.

ideas. Like in the ad *It was the only thing to do after the mule died* from 1971, which many consider one of the campaign's best.

"A lot of the ads that we did were inspired by stories we had heard on the news or read in letters from Beetle owners," Kuperman notes.[4] One day, he and John Noble came across a couple living in a log cabin in the Ozarks, Mr. and Mrs. Hinsley. They had bought a used Beetle after their mule had died. So Kuperman flew out there and asked them to pose for an ad. Initially they refused, thinking that the release that the ad man needed them to sign was a contract to buy their house, their property and their Beetle for 600 dollars. But somehow, Kuperman managed to explain to them that the money was for the right to use their picture in a Volkswagen ad, which they couldn't believe–why would anyone give them 600 dollars just to take their picture in front of their car?

"Anyway," remembers Kuperman, "photographer David Langley and I were finally able to make the shot that we had been assigned to bring home–rather classic, in black-and-white, with Mr. Hinsley and his Volkswagen at a three-quarter angle."[5] They were done when all of a sudden Kuperman had an idea and asked Langley if he carried any color film with him. He did. So Kuperman said, "Let's do another shot, with Mr. Hinsley holding a pitchfork and his wife seated beside him, like in that famous painting by Grant Wood: *American Gothic*."

It was that color shot that became the ad. "This shows you what a great client Volkswagen was," Kuperman remembers. "They didn't care that the picture didn't match the layout. They only cared about the idea and how it could be expressed best."[6]

Alfredo Marcantonio also can't praise Volkswagen enough for its courage:

> *"Just imagine how many clients might have ruined this ad. 'Great, but let's show a pristine, top-of-the-range model. We want to look our best. Hmm … Shouldn't the couple reflect our target audience a bit more closely? Small point: Could the house be rather more aspirational? Mule? Wouldn't pony be nicer? And died … it's so negative.' The result? Two thirtysomethings, outside a country pile with the headline:* It was the only thing to do when the pony was taken ill."[7]

Other ads Kuperman did include *A rare photo*, written by John Noble and featuring a broken-down Beetle being towed off, and *Is nothing sacred?*, written by Bob Levenson and showing a Beetle transformed by its owner into a monster truck.

"All in all, my work was less humorous than Roy Grace's, more competitive," Kuperman says. Like in the ad *Before you look at their new ones, look at their old ones*, featuring a junkyard full of discarded Detroit behemoths. "It took me a year to sell that ad," Kuperman recalls. "Volkswagen was very careful of

A Kuperman ad from 1971. The writer was John Noble.

not bashing too much their U.S. competitors. 'We are only guests here,' they kept saying."[8]

And yet, Kuperman was right when he insisted on positioning the Beetle in a more competitive way. In fact, the Volkswagen campaign would never have become so successful had it not presented a clear enemy–Detroit with its huge gas-guzzlers and the America they stood for. This advertising strategy still works today, think of Apple vs. Microsoft, Virgin vs. British Airways.

"People don't buy WHAT you do," writes marketing guru Simon Sinek, "they buy WHY you do it."[9]

Another effective way of connecting with an audience are so-called 'topical ads' that piggyback on current news events, an approach that DDB pioneered, particularly to the benefit of Volkswagen. This was real-time marketing before the term was coined, based on the idea that when the world's attention has turned to a certain topic, you can grab a piece of attention for your brand.

Another Kuperman ad from 1971,
this time written by Bob Levenson.

This classic was written by Larry
Levenson, Bob Levenson's brother.

Don't forget antifreeze!, warned an ad in the icy winter of 1962, with the subline, "Presented by Volkswagen dealers as a public service to people who don't own cars with air-cooled engines." Len Sirowitz repeated the trick a few years later during a severe drought in New York City with the headline, *Save water*, and the copy, "Presented by Volkswagen, the car with the air-cooled engine that doesn't use any." A third topical classic was *It's ugly, but it gets you there*, in response to the moon landing in 1969, written by Bob Levenson's brother, Larry Levenson, and showing the strange looking Lunar Module *Eagle*.

That same year, Kuperman art directed the most expensive TV commercial Volkswagen had ever done up to that point, again with *Funeral* director Howard Zieff. The spot is set at an auto show in 1949, the year the first Beetles were sold in the U.S. "And now the car of the future, the car the public wants," a presenter cheers as he introduces "the all-new DeSoto."

Later, an announcer in front of the latest Packard is shown ("Your next car for keeps!"), and then a trio of girls sings, "Longer, lower, wider–the 1949 Hudson is the car for you!" Finally, the camera finds a lonely presenter no one seems to notice. He stands in front of an unadorned Beetle and says, "So Volkswagen will constantly be changing, improving and refining this car. Not necessarily to keep in style with the times, but to make a better car. Which means to all of you better mileage." As the camera draws back, a voice-over written by John Noble comments: "Of all the promises made at the 1949 Auto Show, we at Volkswagen kept ours."

True. But alas, Detroit was not the only competition Volkswagen was facing. More and more Americans started trying small and mid-sized cars imported from another World War II foe–Japan. The design of the Datsun Sunny or the Toyota Corolla was new and fresh, they had more interior and trunk space, and their price tag was unbeatable.

To make matters worse, the Beetle started falling short in terms of drive technology, consumption and safety. Sales of the car began to drop, and not even the world's best advertising could stop this. In 1972, just under 486,000 Volkswagens were sold in the U.S., still an impressive number, but almost twenty percent less than in 1970. And the negative trend continued. Slowly, but surely, potential buyers sensed that the Beetle was, in essence, a car from the 1930s.

That's why Wolfsburg started thinking about a replacement. The most successful attempt proved to be the Volkswagen Golf, introduced in 1974 and marketed in the U.S. as the Rabbit. With its angular design and front-wheel-drive, the only thing the Golf and the Beetle had in common was that they were both from Germany. Shortly after, Beetle production at Wolfsburg ended, and in 1976, the last Beetle hardtop was sold in the U.S.

Auto show *from 1969 was the most expensive TV commercial Volkswagen had ever done up to that point. Watch it on tinyurl.com/ugly-autoshow*

The ads for the introduction of the Rabbit were done by the same agency that had been working on the Volkswagen account for over fifteen years–DDB. In fact, the art director of the campaign was Helmut Krone who, for some ads, even worked with his old writing partner Bob Levenson.

There was a good reason for bringing the creative dream team together again: for the first time in the history of their collaboration, Volkswagen was threatening to leave DDB. "We worked all day Friday, all day Saturday, all day Sunday," remembers Jerry Gentile, Krone's assistant at the time. "We were getting bloody noses by the end of the second night because we were just up and constantly working."[10]

The resulting campaign was not bad, by no means. The ad with the headline, *Why we put the engine in sideways*, where Krone set the type sideways, too, shows how brilliant he still was and would continue to be for another decade. And yet, the creative magic seemed to have gone. There was no *Lemon* in the Rabbit campaign and no *Ugly is only skin-deep*, no *Snow Plow* and no *Funeral*. What's more, the campaign didn't pick up the early rumblings of something that no one in the mainstream culture had expressed before. It didn't sense that the tide had turned and cleverly associated itself with the new wave. It didn't leverage a cultural tension to deliver a powerful message.

As, fifteen years earlier, the campaign for the Volkswagen Beetle had done.

CHAPTER 10

"A happy way to live"

How the Volkswagen ads changed more than advertising

N o one in America knows what will happen," the poet Allen Ginsberg wrote in 1959, describing a general sense of disquiet. "No one is in real control."[1] What had caused the alienation?

During the 1950s, consumerism was booming, especially when it came to cars. They really *mattered*, Mary Wells Lawrence remembers, "and success meant, literally, being able to trade in your car for a new model every year, a concept that was kept humming by the Detroit automakers."[2]

This concept was called 'planned obsolescence' and was outlined by GM's Chairman Alfred P. Sloan in the 1920s to assure sales by getting the consumer to *use up* a car instead of using it–i.e. to buy a new car almost as fast as a new toothbrush. This malicious form of consumption engineering wasn't attacked before 1958 when journalist John Keats published *The Insolent Chariots*, accusing Detroit of changing styles every year in order to maximize profits. "It was mere sheet metal cosmetics," remembers Carl H. Hahn. "New tailfins and dashboards instead of true technical progress."[3]

But the spirit of the country began to change as the dissatisfaction with the 'consumption equals happiness' mindset of the 1950s grew. More and more U.S. citizens started to feel that the American Dream was, in fact, a nightmare. "People felt guilty for not being as happy as they were told they should be," author Andrea Hiott writes.[4] The 1950s were "the decade of dazzle, and yet … some began to wonder if any of it had been real."[5]

In 1961, the novel *Revolutionary Road* by Richard Yates perfectly captured the disillusionment of the period. It focused on the hopes and dreams of Frank and April Wheeler, two suburbanites seeking to break out of the lust for conformity and safety that Yates found so characteristic for the 1950s.

Frank has a job at Knox Business Machines, the corporation his father worked at, too–a conservative and bureaucratic company where individualism and creativity are suppressed. One day, April takes Frank's stinging criticism of post-war America (and, yes, Madison Avenue, too) seriously and suggests that they move to France, where she can get a job as a secretary and Frank is able to find more fulfilling work. This way, they would finally free themselves from the suburban routine and small-mindedness that must surely cause their malaise. Their plans to leave the U.S. begin to fall apart when April discovers that she's pregnant with their third child, and Frank begins to resign himself to his boring job at the prospect of a promotion. After an argument with her husband, April–haunted by the ghosts of a troubled childhood–tries to self-abort her child and eventually dies from blood loss. Frank, feeling deeply guilty, is left a shattered wreck of a man, epitomizing the despair of a lot of post-war Americans who started finding the materialist pursuit of happiness fruitless, and the American Dream to be hollow and deceptive.

DDB was clever enough to sense this psychological sea change, and appealed with the VW campaign to the longing for individuality in a wildly conforming society. By buying a Volkswagen, Julian Koenig said in an interview from 1992, "you could take an inverse delight in not having to keep up with the Jones' … in not being part of that repetitive, competitive culture."[6] "Over the years almost

Live below your means.

If you'd like to get around the high cost of living, we have a suggestion:
Cut down on the high cost of getting around.
And buy a Volkswagen. It's only $1799*.
That's around $1200 less than the average amount paid for a new car today. (Leave it in the bank. More's coming.)

A VW saves you hundreds of dollars on upkeep over the years.
It takes pints, not quarts, of oil.
Not one iota of antifreeze.
And it gets about 27 miles to the gallon. The average car (thirsty devil that it is) only gets 14.
So the more you drive, the more you save.

And chances are, you'll drive it for years and years. (Since we never change the style, a VW never goes out of style.)
Of course, a VW's not much to look at. So a lot of people buy a big flashy car just to save face.
Try putting that in the bank.

Ad after ad (as in this one from 1968), DDB's campaign for the Beetle contributed to the cultural change of the 1960s—away from the materialism and conformism of the post-war years.

every part in the Volkswagen has been changed (but not its heart or face)," Koenig wrote in *What year car do the Jones* [sic] *drive?*, one of the early VW ads. And he continued: "Volkswagen owners find this a happy way to drive–and to live."

Ad after ad, DDB's campaign for the Beetle contributed to the cultural change of the 1960s–away from the materialism and conformism of the post-war years, towards, ultimately, the idealism and individualism of the hippies. In fact, by acknowledging the growing critique of the 'bigger is better' mindset, the Volkswagen campaign served as a translator between the underground rejection of the American Way of Life expressed by the Beatniks–novelists and poets such as Jack Kerouac (*On the Road*, published in 1957) and William S. Burroughs (*Naked Lunch*, published in 1959)–and the mainstream cultural revolution of the 1960s.

Just from reading the ads, analyzed agency founder Scott Goodson, you got "some sense of the people who made [them], as well as the people who made the car."[7] They were zigging while all others were zagging. "In a time of conformity and 'keeping up with the Joneses,' [these ads were] about going your own way."[8]

In fact, you could even argue that the Volkswagen campaign turned Allen Ginsberg's famous poem *Howl* from 1956 into ads. Since Detroit's policy was not just to manufacture cars, but to manufacture discontent with the one you had just bought last year, Volkswagen and DDB took direct aim at that system. "They 'manufactured discontent' with the system of 'manufacturing discontent,'" as author Phil Patton puts it.[9] They grew the number of Americans who didn't want a rolling advertisement for consumerism anymore, and thereby actually drove cultural change.

A fact as unique as the Volkswagen campaign itself, because advertising had–and has–always been about the *confirmation* of

As illustrated by this ad from 1970, the Beetle became a protest sign on wheels, an icon of the counterculture.

values, not about their deconstruction, featuring women who weren't mothers, black businessmen or self-confident gays only long after they were accepted by society.

According to Julian Koenig, all this was not intended. "I've always objected to the materialism of the American Way of Life," he said, "and of course I was attacking Detroit by making the Volkswagen the antithesis of planned obsolescence. But *Think small* and the other ads that I did were not created to create a different society. I only wanted to position the Volkswagen as distinctly as possible, not tear down the establishment."[10]

For Koenig, the Beetle was the car for the cultural intelligentsia, a positioning strategy that Carl H. Hahn fully supported. "We wanted to make the Volkswagen a symbol of a completely different consumer philosophy," he notes.[11] The VW ads not only made the Beetle the clever choice—you simply had more taste when you bought a Volkswagen. Phil Patton, again, brings it to the point: "Beetle ownership allowed you to show off that you didn't need to show off."[12] (On a philosophical side note: by making the resistance to consumerism a selling point,

97

DDB turned dissent into just another commodity. A curious irony of the Volkswagen campaign: a leftist–at some time in his life even Marxist–copywriter causes total capitalism through his defiance of consumerism.)

In short, the VW campaign did more than create a successful product–it created a cultural phenomenon. The Volkswagen became a protest sign on wheels, an icon of the counterculture. Flowers and peace signs were painted all over it. Only one other car was as popular with the freewheelin' hippies–the bigger brother of the Beetle, the VW Bus, whose advertising also came from DDB.

What a proof for the power of creativity: a car designed for the masses becomes a symbol of the critique of mass society; a car designed for the Nazis becomes the preferred automobile of the Peace Generation.

What made this possible? What made the Volkswagen campaign so powerful that it ultimately resonated way beyond DDB's intentions?

Dave Reider, one of the early writers on the VW campaign, was self-confident enough to see a quasi-Hegelian *Weltgeist* responsible for this: "I think that every time in history has a group of individuals who best capture the spirit of that time," he boldly declared, "like Shakespeare and Johnson and Marlowe at the Mermaid Tavern, or the Algonquin Round Table group … I think for now, it's us."[13]

A more profane explanation would be to say that the enormous impact of the VW campaign was merely a lucky coincidence: the Beetle was such a radically different car that the only way to sell it was through utter honesty, and this utter honesty appealed to the 1960s' growing counterculture.

The stars aligned. It was the right campaign for the right product at the right time.

EPILOGUE

When *Advertising Age* picked its top 100 campaigns ever, it chose the one for the Volkswagen as the very best, and so did *Time Magazine* in its Millennium edition. Both a leading trade journal and a leading popular magazine thus acknowledged that no other ad campaign has been so creative, so influential and, last but not least, so effective. After all, the VW ads helped turn a relict of Nazi Germany into the pinnacle of lovability–could advertising ever achieve more?

What makes the campaign even more unique is the fact that the writers and art directors who created it, the account executives who helped produce it and the advertising managers at Volkswagen who approved it didn't have any tried and tested marketing recipes to follow, no New York Art Directors Annuals to steal from.

Instead of standing on the shoulders of giants, they had to become giants themselves.

And yet, there's a question one can rightly ask: is a campaign started almost sixty years ago still relevant today? Isn't it a mere trip down memory lane, a wistful recollection of the Golden Age of Advertising?

A somewhat philosophical answer would be that to find a way forward, you need to know your roots; to have a future, you need to know your past. But studying the Volkswagen campaign is much more relevant than that. It is an impressive lesson about the virtues of courage, simplicity and wit.

And most of all, it is a lesson in acknowledging the true place of advertising in people's lives.

The fact is: ads are annoying. Nobody–*nobody*–waits for them, and lots of people even actively avoid them. It's easy to understand why: ads interrupt the editorial content, the radio show or the TV series we're enjoying. They pop up on websites and spoil landscapes.

That's why advertising must do more than simply try to get people's attention–it must try to get their respect. And there's only one way to achieve this: by deeply acknowledging that advertising is, at its core, a nuisance.

The Volkswagen campaign took this fact into account like no other campaign before, and with its hundreds of executions, it did this longer than any other campaign after.

Each ad wasn't only created to sell the Beetle–it also set out to prove that advertising has a right to exist, because, fundamentally, it is born lacking one. And there's something else that makes the Volkswagen campaign still valuable: it is a testimony to the fact that advertising can be more than a business model–but a way to make a dent in the universe. "All of us who professionally use the mass media are the shapers of society," Bill Bernbach said. "We can vulgarize that society. We can brutalize it. Or we can help lift it onto a higher level."[1]

This strong correlation between being creative and being socially conscious is an important point about the Creative Revolution that tends to get overlooked. Bill Bernbach, Julian Koenig, Bob Levenson, Len Sirowitz, Bob Kuperman–they were all 'ethnics' who not only wanted to change the WASPy advertising of their time, but its WASPy society, too. Their fight against the advertising establishment was also a fight against the political, cultural and moral establishment.

And they won. They helped make the U.S. a freer and more colorful place.

Fifty years later, the advertising community isn't interested in social commitment anymore, unless there is a

The Volkswagen campaign in a 1984 exhibition of Helmut Krone's work at the Art Center College of Design in Pasadena, California.

coveted creative award to be won. In this case, a charitable organization with no money will grant an agency carte blanche for a campaign whose primary aim is to impress other ad creatives. The few ad men who actually still get involved in social causes sooner or later turn their back on agency life, as the former U.S. star creative Alex Bogusky did who now pursues sustainability projects.

Maybe this is the final reason why the Volkswagen campaign is revered to this day: it is the poignant memory of a time when advertising wasn't mostly ignored, but, literally, moved the world.

★★★

NOTES

CHAPTER 1

1. Cummings, p 40
2. Ibid., p 41–42
3. Fox, p 253
4. Ibid.
5. Imseng, Lois
6. Ross
7. Ibid.
8. Gage
9. Higgins, p 108
10. Imseng, Marcantonio
11. Higgins, p 20
12. Levenson, p XVI–XVII
13. Wells Lawrence, p 6
14. Dusenberry, p 246–247
15. Willens, p 40
16. One. A Magazine

CHAPTER 2

1. Nishio, Robinson
2. Tungate, p 52
3. Della Femina, p 2–3
4. Dusenberry, p 246–247
5. Imseng, Marcantonio
6. One. A Magazine
7. Delaney, p 12
8. One. A Magazine
9. Wells Lawrence, p 6
10. Imseng, Levenson

11. Tungate, p 50
12. Feldwick, p 89
13. One. A Magazine
14. Delaney, p 12
15. Rowsome, p 65
16. Levenson, Bernbach's Book, p 19

CHAPTER 3

1. Kiley, p 48
2. Price, p 50
3. Ingrassia, p 109
4. Harrison, p 41
5. Imseng, Hahn
6. Ibid.
7. Ibid.
8. Ibid.
9. Nelson, p 217
10. Ibid., p 217–218
11. Ibid., p 218
12. Ibid.
13. Ibid.
14. Imseng, Hahn

CHAPTER 4

1. Imseng, Hahn
2. Nelson, p 218–219
3. Copping, p 42
4. Fox, p 200
5. Krone, Smithsonian talk
6. Tungate, p 54
7. Imseng, Kuperman
8. Krone, Archive
9. Imseng, Koenig

10. Ibid.
11. Ibid.
12. Ibid.
13. Herzbrun, p 63
14. Imseng, Kuperman
15. Mack
16. Imseng, Lois
17. Imseng, Koenig
18. Karl
19. Imseng, Koenig
20. Challis, p 70
21. Ibid., p 64
22. Nelson, p 216
23. Imseng, Hahn
24. Rowsome, p 73–74
25. Kahn, p 308
26. Imseng, Trott
27. Imseng, Heller
28. Karl
29. Imseng, Lois
30. Imseng, Koenig
31. Ibid.
32. Rowsome, p 90–91
33. Challis, p 69
34. Ibid.
35. Imseng, Hahn

CHAPTER 5

1. Advertising Age
2. Challis, p 68
3. Imseng, Koenig
4. Imseng, Lois
5. Ibid.

6. Karl
7. Cooke
8. Imseng, Koenig
9. Heller, p 564
10. Kaplan, p 55
11. Ries
12. Imseng, Hahn
13. Imseng, Trott

CHAPTER 6

1. Imseng, Levenson
2. Krone, Archive
3. Imseng, Levenson
4. Imseng, Hahn
5. Challis, p 70
6. Karl
7. Imseng, Trott
8. Challis, p 68
9. Imseng, Levenson
10. Rowsome, p 82
11. Levenson, p 217
12. Krone, Archive
13. Hiott, p 265

CHAPTER 7

1. Imseng, Sirowitz
2. Ibid.
3. Ibid.
4. Challis, p 63
5. Ibid., p 73
6. Imseng, Lois
7. Imseng, Marcantonio
8. Ibid.

9. Ibid.
10. Imseng, Sirowitz
11. Imseng, Lois
12. Imseng, Koenig
13. Imseng, Levenson
14. Imseng, Lois
15. Imseng, Hahn
16. Nishio, Levenson
17. Barden/Morgan, p 6
18. Ibid., p 15

CHAPTER 8

1. Herzbrun, p 97
2. Imseng, Sirowitz
3. Imseng, Kuperman
4. Nishio, Noble
5. Aitchison, p 151
6. Ibid.
7. Kiley, p 101
8. Hilliard, p 92
9. Aitchison, p 159
10. Imseng, Trott
11. Marcantonio, p 10
12. Ingrassia, p 100
13. Hoffman

CHAPTER 9

1. Imseng, McCabe
2. Imseng, Kuperman
3. Ibid.
4. Ibid.
5. Ibid.
6. Ibid.

7. Marcantonio, Not a lemon
8. Imseng, Kuperman
9. Sinek, p 42
10. Challis, p 167

CHAPTER 10

1. Hiott, p 5
2. Wells Lawrence, p 7
3. Imseng, Hahn
4. Hiott, p 267
5. Ibid., p 5
6. Mack
7. Goodson, p 28
8. Ibid.
9. Patton, p 102
10. Imseng, Koenig
11. Imseng, Hahn
12. Patton, p 104
13. Herzbrun, p 67

EPILOGUE

1. Cracknell, p 13

SOURCES

Abbott, David & Marcantonio, Alfredo & O'Driscoll, John: Remember Those Great Volkswagen Ads? Merrell Publishers, 2014 (The ultimate collection of Volkswagen ads.)

Ad Age Advertising Century: Top 100 Campaigns. tinyurl. com/qbejqfh

Barden, Mark & Morgan, Adam: A Beautiful Constraint. How To Transform Your Limitations Into Advantages, and Why It's Everyone's Business. Wiley, 2015

Berger, Warren: When Ads Got Smart. In: Advertising Today. Phaidon, 2001, p 42–81

Challis, Clive: Helmut Krone. The Book. Graphic Design and Art Direction (Concept, Form and Meaning) After Advertising's Creative Revolution. The Cambridge Enchorial Press, 2005 (The ultimate book on Helmut Krone.)

Cooke, Marty: Was Helmut Krone a Genius? tinyurl.com/z7fgynl

Copping, Richard: VW Advertising. The Art of Advertising the Air-Cooled Volkswagen. Herridge & Sons, 2014

Cracknell, Andrew: The Real Mad Men. The Renegades of Madison Avenue and the Golden Age of Advertising. Running Press, 2012

Cummings, Bart: The Benevolent Dictators. Interviews with Advertising Greats. Crain Books, 1984

DDB News: A Conversation with Ned Doyle. tinyurl.com/26vwmea

Delaney, Sam: Get Smashed. The Story of the Men Who Made the Adverts That Changed Our Lives. Sceptre, 2007

Della Femina, Jerry: From Those Wonderful Folks Who Gave You Pearl Harbor. Front-Line Dispatches from the Advertising War. Simon and Schuster Paperbacks, 2010

Dobrow, Larry: When Advertising Tried Harder. The Sixties: The Golden Age of American Advertising. Friendly Press, 1984

Dusenberry, Phil: One Great Insight Is Worth a Thousand Good Ideas. An Advertising Hall-of-Famer Reveals the Most Powerful Secret in Business. Portfolio, 2005

Feldwick, Paul: The Anatomy of Humbug. How to Think Differently about Advertising. Troubador Publishing, 2015

Fox, Stephen: The Mirror Makers. A History of American Advertising and Its Creators. Vintage Books, 1985

Frank, Thomas: The Conquest of Cool. Business Culture, Counterculture and the Rise of Hip Consumerism. The University of Chicago Press, 1997

Gage, Bob: "I Love Advertisements." tinyurl.com/ygna5cw

Glatzer, Robert: The New Advertising. The Great Campaigns from Avis to Volkswagen. Citadel Press, 1970

Goodson, Scott: Uprising. How to Build a Brand–and Change the World–By Sparking Cultural Movements. Mcgraw-Hill, 2012

Harrison, Steve: Changing the World Is the Only Fit Work for a Grown Man. Adworld Press, 2012

Heimann, Jim & Heller, Steve: Mid-Century Ads. Taschen, 2015

Herzbrun, David: Playing in Traffic on Madison Avenue. Tales of Advertising's Glory Years. Dow Jones-Irwin, 1990

Higgins, Denis: The Art of Writing Advertising. Conversations with William Bernbach, George Gribbin, Rosser Reeves, David Ogilvy and Leo Burnett. McGraw-Hill, 2003

Hilliard, Robert: Writing for Television, Radio and New Media. Wadsworth, 2011

Hiott, Andrea: Thinking Small. The Long, Strange Trip of the Volkswagen Beetle. Ballantine Books, 2012

Hoffman, Bob: Volkswagen Will Be Saved By Its Advertising. tinyurl.com/j265hme

Imseng, Dominik: Conversations with Carl H. Hahn in June 2010 and January 2015

Imseng, Dominik: Conversation with Steven Heller in February 2016

Imseng, Dominik: Conversation with Julian Koenig in February 2010

Imseng, Dominik: Conversation with Bob Kuperman in January 2015

Imseng, Dominik: Conversation with Bob Levenson in June 2010

Imseng, Dominik: Conversation with George Lois in June 2009

Imseng, Dominik: Conversation with Alfredo Marcantonio in March 2013

Imseng, Dominik: Conversation with Ed McCabe in June 2015

Imseng, Dominik: Conversation with Len Sirowitz in January 2015

Imseng, Dominik: Conversation with Dave Trott in June 2015

Ingrassia, Paul: Engines of Change. A History of the American Dream in Fifteen Cars. Simon & Schuster, 2012

Jackall, Robert & Hirota, Janice M.: Image Makers.

Advertising, Public Relations and the Ethos of Advocacy. The University of Chicago Press, 2000

Kahn, Eve M.: Ad Campaign of the Century. In: Graphic Design History. Edited by Steven Heller and Georgette Ballance. Allworth Press, 2001, p 305–310

Kaplan, Fred: 1959: The Year Everything Changed. Wiley, 2010

Karl, Sandra: An Interview with Helmut Krone. tinyurl.com/ye4audj

Kiley, David: Getting the Bugs Out. The Rise, Fall and Comeback of Volkswagen in America. John Wiley & Sons, 2002

Krone, Helmut: Talk at the Smithsonian Institution in Washington, D.C., on November 15, 1982 (courtesy of Kate Krone)

Krone, Helmut: Various unlabeled talks and notes from his personal archive (courtesy of Kate Krone)

Levenson, Bob: Bill Bernbach At 100. tinyurl.com/nwzjbkj

Levenson, Bob: Bill Bernbach's Book. A History of the Advertising That Changed the History of Advertising. Villard, 1987

Lois, George: George, Be Careful. A Greek Florist's Kid in the Roughhouse World of Advertising. Saturday Review Press, 1972

Mack, Joanna: Without Walls–Heil Herbie. tinyurl.com/y497tev

Marcantonio, Alfredo & O'Driscoll, John: Not a Lemon in the Bunch. tinyurl.com/pacxly9

Nelson, Walter Henry: Small Wonder. The Amazing Story of the Volkswagen. Little, Brown and Company, 1970

Nishio, Tadahisa: An Interview with Robert Levenson. tinyurl.com/mexew6m

Nishio, Tadahisa: An Interview with John Noble. tinyurl. com/kgpna5b

Nishio, Tadahisa: An Interview with Phyllis Robinson. tinyurl.com/ybtqkm6

One. A Magazine: Reliving the Revolution. tinyurl.com/ yl6mf2x

O'Reilly, Terry & Tennant, Mike: The Age of Persuasion. How Marketing Ate Our Culture. Counterpoint, 2010

Packard, Vance: The Hidden Persuaders. Ig Publishing, 2007

Patton, Phil: Bug. The Strange Mutations of the World's Most Famous Automobile. Simon & Schuster, 2002

Price, Ryan Lee: The VW Beetle. A Production History of the World's Most Famous Car, 1936–1967. HP Books, 2003

Reeves, Rosser: Reality in Advertising. Mac Gibbon & Kee, 1961

Rieger, Bernhard: The People's Car. A Global History of the Volkswagen Beetle. Harvard University Press, 2013

Ries, Al: Advertising Could Do With More of Bernbach's Genius. tinyurl.com/lwv3joc

Ross, Randall: Mechanized Mules of Victory. tinyurl.com/ m2qqd4h

Rowsome, Frank, Jr.: Think Small. The Story of Those Volkswagen Ads. The Stephen Greene Press, 1970

Russell, Peter & Slingerland, Senta: Game Changers. The Evolution of Advertising. Taschen, 2013

Sinek, Simon: Start with Why. How Great Leaders Inspire Everyone to Take Action. Portfolio, 2011

Sivulka, Juliann: Soap, Sex and Cigarettes. A Cultural History of American Advertising. Wadsworth, 1998

Tungate, Mark: Adland. A Global History of Advertising. Kogan Page, 2007

Twitchell, James B.: Twenty Ads That Shook the World. The Century's Most Groundbreaking Advertising and How It Changed Us All. Three Rivers Press, 2000

Vargas-Cooper, Natasha: Mad Men Unbuttoned. A Romp Through 1960s America. Collins Design, 2010

Vaske, Hermann: Standing on the Shoulders of Giants. Conversations with the Masters of Advertising. Die Gestalten Verlag, 2001

Wells Lawrence, Mary: A Big Life in Advertising. Knopf, 2002

Willens, Doris: Nobody's Perfect. Bill Bernbach and the Golden Age of Advertising. CreateSpace, 2009

URLs last checked on July 14, 2016

PICTURE CREDITS

FOREWORD

Carl H. Hahn. Volkswagen.

INTRODUCTION

Amir Kassaei. DDB.

CHAPTER 1

Bill Bernbach. DDB.
Paul Rand. Paul-Rand.com.
Direction cover. Paul-Rand.com.
Dubonnet ad. Paul-Rand.com.
Phyllis Robinson and Bob Gage. Eddie Hausner/
The New York Times.
Rosser Reeves. Ted Bates Inc.
Anacin ad. Ted Bates Inc.
Newspaper clipping. DDB.

CHAPTER 2

Bill Bernbach. DDB.
Ohrbach's ad. DDB.
Levy's ad. DDB.
El Al ad. DDB.

CHAPTER 3

Adolf Hitler. Heinrich Hoffmann/Getty Images.
Ferdinand Porsche. Keystone/Getty Images.
Kübelwagen. Deutsches Bundesarchiv/Picture 101I-786-

0305-19/Photographer: Otto.
Heinz Nordhoff. Volkswagen.
Hans Looser ad. Volkswagen.
Carl H. Hahn. Volkswagen.
El Al ad. DDB.
Polaroid ad. DDB.

CHAPTER 4

Helmut Schmitz, Bill Bernbach, Carl H. Hahn,
Ned Doyle. Volkswagen.
The Hidden Persuaders cover. Penguin Books.
Helmut Krone. Kate Krone.
Julian Koenig. Papert Koenig Lois.
Lincoln ad. The Lincoln Motor Company.
Bernd Reuters ad. Volkswagen.

CHAPTER 5

George Lois. George Lois.

CHAPTER 6

Bob Levenson. DDB.
Bill Bernbach obituary ad. DDB.

CHAPTER 7

Len Sirowitz. DDB.

CHAPTER 8

Roy Grace. DDB.
Levy's ads. DDB.

CHAPTER 9

Bob Kuperman. DDB.

EPILOGUE

Helmut Krone exhibition. Kate Krone.

ACKNOWLEDGEMENTS

Helmut Krone. Kate Krone.

All Volkswagen ads are reproduced by kind permission of Volkswagen and DDB.

INDEX

ACKNOWLEDGEMENTS

I would like to thank the many advertising greats who generously took the time to talk with me for this book: the late Julian Koenig, Bob Kuperman, the late Bob Levenson, George Lois, Alfredo Marcantonio, Ed McCabe, Len Sirowitz as well as Dave Trott. I would also like to thank Carl H. Hahn for the extensive conversations we had and for writing a wonderful foreword. Thanks to Amir Kassaei, too, for his inspiring introduction, and to Kate Krone who kindly let me access her dad's archive.

A final big thank you goes to copywriting legend and master advertising historian Steve Harrison who had a last hard look at the manuscript.

Dominik Imseng   *July 14, 2016*

Helmut Krone (1925–1996), the 'art director's art director.'

ABOUT THE AUTHOR

Dominik Imseng (b. 1968) received a M.A. in Philosophy, German Literature and History of Art from the University of Zurich. He works as a copywriter and journalist in Switzerland and regularly interviews advertising greats.

Dominik has never owned a Volkswagen Beetle. In fact, he doesn't even know how to drive. Feel free to get in touch with him (and maybe even book him for a talk about the Volkswagen campaign): dimseng@me.com

How to do a Volkswagen ad.

1. Look at the car.

2. Look harder. You'll find enough advantages to fill a lot of ads. Like the air-cooled engine, the economy, the design that never goes out of date.

3. Don't exaggerate. For instance, some people have gotten 50 m.p.g. and more from a VW. But others have only managed 28. Average: 32. Don't promise more.

4. Call a spade a spade. And a suspension a suspension. Not something like "orbital cushioning."

5. Speak to the reader. Don't shout. He can hear you. Especially if you talk sense.

6. Pencil sharp? You're on your own.

(Picture goes here.)

(Write headline here.)

(Start copy here.)

(Picture goes here.)

_____

(Write headline here.)

(Start copy here.)

(Picture goes here.)

(Write headline here.)

(Start copy here.)

VW

(Picture goes here.)

(Write headline here.)

(Start copy here.)